A
MEDITATIVE
COMMENTARY
ON THE
NEW TESTAMENT

1 & 2 THESSALONIANS, 1 & 2 TIMOTHY AND TITUS:

JESUS GROWS HIS CHURCH

by Gary Holloway

LEAFWOOD
PUBLISHERS

1 & 2 THESSALONIANS, 1 & 2 TIMOTHY AND TITUS:
JESUS GROWS HIS CHURCH

Published by Leafwood Publishers

Copyright 2006 by Gary Holloway

ISBN 0-89112-503-5
Printed in the United States of America

Cover & interior design by Greg Jackson, Thinkpen Design

For information:
Leafwood Publishers
1648 Campus Court
Abilene, Texas 79601
1-877-816-4455 (toll free)

Visit our website: www.leafwoodpublishers.com

06 07 08 09 10 / 7 6 5 4 3 2 1

To Mike and Sandy Nonnenmacher,
who lovingly pass on the faith to the next generation

C O N T E N T S

INTRODUCTION

HEARING GOD IN SCRIPTURE

There are many commentaries, guides, and workbooks on the various books of the Bible. How is this series different? It is not intended to answer all your scholarly questions about the Bible, or even make you an expert in the details of Scripture. Instead, this series is designed to help you hear the voice of God for your everyday life. It is a guide to meditation on the Bible, meditation that will allow the Bible to transform you.

We read in many ways. We might scan the newspaper for information, read a map for location, read a novel for pleasure, or read a textbook to pass a test. These are all good ways to read, depending on our circumstances.

A young soldier far away from home who receives a letter from his wife reads in yet another way. He might scan the letter quickly at first for news and information. But his longing for his beloved causes him to read the letter again and again, hearing her sweet voice in every line. He slowly treasures each word of this precious letter.

BIBLE STUDY

So also, there are many good ways to read the Bible, depending on our circumstances. Bible study is absolutely necessary for our life with God. We rightly study the Bible for information. We ask, "Who wrote this?" "When was it written?" "Who were the original readers?" "How do these words apply to me?" More importantly, we want information about God. Who is he? What does he think of me? What does he want from me?

There is no substitute for this kind of close, dedicated Bible study. We must know what the Bible says to know our standing with God. We therefore read the Bible to discover true doctrine or teaching. But some in their emphasis on the authority and inspiration of the Bible have forgotten that Bible study is not an end in itself. We want to know God through Scripture. We want to have a relationship with the Teacher, not just the teachings.

Jesus tells some of God's people in his day, "You diligently study the Scriptures because you think that by them you possess eternal life. These are the Scriptures that testify about me, yet you refuse to come to me to have life" (John 5:39-40). He's not telling them to study their Bibles less, but he is reminding them of the deeper purpose of Bible study—to draw us to God through Jesus. Bible study is a means, not an end.

Yet the way many of us have learned to study the Bible may actually get in the way of hearing God. "Bible study" may sound a lot like schoolwork, and many of us were happy to get out of school. "Bible study" may call to mind pictures of intellectuals surrounded by books in Greek and Hebrew, pondering meanings too deep for ordinary people. The method of Bible study that has been popular for some time focuses on the strangeness of the Bible. It was written long ago, far away, and in languages we cannot read. There is a huge gap between us and the original readers of the Bible, a gap that can only be bridged by scholars, not by average folk.

There is some truth and some value in that "scholarly"method. It is true that the Bible was not written originally to us. Knowing ancient languages and customs can at times help us understand the Bible better. However, one unintended result of this approach is to make the Bible distant from the people of God. We may come to think that we can only hear God indirectly through Scripture, that his word must be filtered through scholars. We may even think that deep Bible study is a matter of mastering obscure information about the Bible.

Meditation

But we read the Bible for more than information. By studying it, we experience transformation, the mysterious process of God at work in us. Through his loving words, God is calling us to life with him. He is forming us into the image of his Son.

Reading the Bible is not like reading other books. We are not simply trying to learn information or master material. Instead, we want to stand under the authority of Scripture and let God master us. While we read the Bible, it reads us, opening the depths of our being to the overpowering love of God. "For the word of God is living and active. Sharper than any double-edged sword, it penetrates even to dividing soul and spirit, joints and marrow; it judges the thoughts and attitudes of the heart. Nothing in all creation is hidden from God's sight. Everything is uncovered and laid bare before the eyes of him to whom we must give account" (Hebrews 4:12-13).

Opening our hearts to the word of God is meditation. Although this way of reading the Bible may be new to some, it has a long heritage among God's people. The Psalmist joyously meditates on the words of God (Psalm 1:2; 39:3; 119:15, 23, 27, 48, 78, 97, 99, 148). Meditation is taking the words of Scripture to heart and letting them ask questions of us. It is slowing chewing over a text, listening closely, reading God's message of love to us over and over. This is not a simple, easy, or naïve reading of Scripture, but a process that takes time, dedication, and practice on our part.

There are many ways to meditate on the Bible. One is praying the Scriptures. Prayer and Bible study really cannot be separated. One way of praying the Bible is to make the words of a text your prayer. Obviously, the prayer texts of Scripture, especially the Psalms, lend themselves to this. "The Lord is my shepherd" has been the prayer of many hearts.

However, it is proper and helpful to turn the words of the Bible into prayers. Commands from God can become prayers. "You shall have no other gods before me" (Exodus 20:3) can be prayed, "Lord, keep me from anything that takes your place in my heart." Stories can be prayed. Jesus heals a man born blind (John 9), and so we pray, "Lord Jesus open my eyes to who you truly are." Even the promises of the Bible become prayers. "Never will I leave you; never will I forsake you" (Deuteronomy 31:6; Hebrews 13:5) becomes "God help me know that you promise that you are always with me and so live my life without fear."

Obviously, there are many helpful ways of hearing the voice of God in Scripture. Again, the purpose of Bible reading and study is not to know more about the Bible, much less to pride ourselves as experts on Scripture. Instead, we read to hear the voice of our Beloved. We listen for a word of God for us.

Holy Reading

This commentary reflects one ancient way of meditation and praying the Scriptures known as lectio divina or holy reading. This method assumes that God wants to speak to us directly in the Bible, that the passage we are reading is God's word to us right now. The writers of the New Testament read the Old Testament with this same conviction. They saw the words of the Bible speaking directly to their own situation. They read with humility and with prayer.

The first step along this way of holy reading is listening to the Bible. Choose a biblical text that is not too long. This commentary breaks these biblical letters into smaller sections. The purpose is to hear God's voice in your current situation, not to cover material or prepare lessons. Get into a comfortable position and maintain silence before God for several minutes. This prepares the heart to listen. Read slowly. Savor each word. Perhaps read aloud. Listen for a particular phrase that speaks to you. Ask God, "What are you trying to tell me today?"

The next step is to meditate on that particular phrase. That meditation may include slowly repeating the phrase that seems to be for you today. As you think deeply on it, you might even memorize it. Committing biblical passages to memory allows us to hold them in our hearts all day long. If you keep a journal, you might write the passage there. Let those words sink deeply into your heart.

Then pray those words back to God in your heart. Those words may call up visual images, smells, sounds, and feelings. Pay attention to what God is giving you in those words. Then respond in faith to what those words say to your heart. What do they call you to be and to do? Our humble response might take the form of praise, thanksgiving, joy, confession, or even cries of pain.

The final step in this "holy reading" is contemplation of God. The words from God that we receive deeply in our hearts lead us to him. Through these words, we experience union with the all-powerful God of love. Again, one should not separate Bible reading from prayer. The words of God in Scripture transport us into the very presence of God where we joyfully rest in his love.

What keeps reading the Bible this way from becoming merely our own desires read back into Scripture? How do we know it is God's voice we hear and not our own?

Two things. One is prayer. We are asking God to open our hearts, minds, and lives to him. We ask to hear his voice, not ours and not the voice of the world around us.

The second thing that keeps this from being an exercise in self-deception is to study the Bible in community. By praying over

Scripture in a group, we hear God's word together. God speaks through the other members of our group. The wisdom he gives them keeps us from private, selfish, and unusual interpretations. They help us keep our own voices in check, as we desire to listen to God alone.

HOW TO USE THIS COMMENTARY

This commentary provides assistance in holy reading of the Bible. It gives structure to daily personal devotions, family meditation, small group Bible studies, and church classes.

DAILY DEVOTIONAL

Listening, meditation, prayer, contemplation. How does this commentary fit into this way of Bible study? Consider it as a conversation partner. We have taken a section of Scripture and then broken it down into four short daily readings. After listening, meditating, praying, and contemplating the passage for the day, use the questions suggested in the commentary to provoke deeper reflection. This provides a structure for a daily fifteen minute devotional four days a week. On the fifth day, read the entire passage, meditate, and then use the questions to reflect on the meaning of the whole. On day six, take our meditations on the passage as conversation with another who has prayed over the text.

If you want to begin daily Bible reading, but need guidance, this provides a Monday-Saturday experience that prepares the heart for worship and praise on Sunday. This structure also results in a communal reading of Scripture, instead of a private reading. Even if you use this commentary alone, you are not reading privately. God is at work in you and in the conversation you have with another (the author of the commentary) who has sought to hear God through this passage of the Bible.

FAMILY BIBLE STUDY

This commentary can also provide an arrangement for family Bible study. Many Christian parents want to lead their children in daily study, but don't know where to begin or how to structure their time. Using the six-day plan outlined above means the entire family can read, meditate, pray, and reflect on the shorter passages, using the questions provided. On day five, they can review the entire passage, and then on day six, read the meditations in the commentary to prompt reflection and discussion. God will bless our families beyond our imaginations through the prayerful study of his word.

WEEKLY GROUP STUDY

This commentary can also structure small group Bible study. Each member of the group should have meditated over the daily readings and questions for the five days preceding the group meeting, using the method outlined above. The day before the group meeting, each member should read and reflect on the meditations in the commentary on that passage. You then can meet once a week to hear God's word together. In that group meeting, the method of holy reading would look something like this:

Listening
1) Five minutes of silence.
2) Slow reading of the biblical passage for that week.
3) A minute of silent meditation on the passage.
4) Briefly share with the group the word or phrase that struck you.

Personal Message

    5) A second reading of the same passage.

    6) A minute of silence.

    7) Where does this touch your life today?

    8) Responses: I hear, I see, etc.

Life Response

    9) Brief silence.

    10) What does God want you to do today in light of this word?

Group Prayer

    11) Have each member of the group pray aloud for the person on his or her left, asking God to bless the word he has given them.

The procedure suggested here can be used in churches or in neighborhood Bible studies. Church members would use the daily readings Monday-Friday in their daily devotionals. This commentary intentionally provides no readings on the sixth day, so that we can spend Saturdays as a time of rest, not rest from Bible study, but a time to let God's word quietly work its way deep into our hearts. Sunday during Bible school or in home meetings, the group would meet to experience the weekly readings together, using the group method described above. It might be that the sermon for each Sunday could be on the passage for that week.

There are churches that have used this structure to great advantage. In the hallways of those church buildings, the talk is not of the local football team or the weather, but of the shared experience of the Word of God for that week.

And that is the purpose of our personal and communal study, to hear the voice of God, our loving Father who wants us to love him in return. He deeply desires a personal relationship with us. Father, Son, and Spirit make a home inside us (see John 14:16-17, 23). Our loving God speaks to his children! But we must listen for his voice. That listening is not a matter of gritting our teeth and trying harder to hear. Instead, it is part of our entire life with God. That is what Bible study is all about.

Through daily personal prayer and meditation on God's word and through a communal reading of Scripture, our most important conversation partner, the Holy Spirit, will do his mysterious and marvelous work. Among other things, the Spirit pours God's love into our hearts (Romans 5:5), bears witness to our spirits that we are God's children (Romans 8:16), intercedes for us with God (Romans 8:26), and enlightens us as to God's will (Ephesians 1:17).

So this is an invitation to personal daily Bible study, to praying the Scriptures, to sharing with fellow believers, to hear the voice of God. God will bless us, our families, our churches, and his world if we take the time to be still, listen, and do his word.

1 THESSALONIANS: JESUS IS FAITHFUL

THE SPIRITUALITY OF 1 THESSALONIANS

Paul writes this letter to a church he started then abruptly had to leave. As a result, he is concerned about the depth of their faith. Would they think that God's messenger had abandoned them and reject the message he brought? No! They are faithful in Paul's absence, because they truly trust the good news of Jesus.

The spirituality of 1 Thessalonians is thus a very practical spirituality, concerned with faithful living each day.

A Spiritual Message

It is often hard to continue to believe the message of Jesus when bad times come. The Thessalonians accepted the message Paul brought, the good news of Jesus, as a word from God. It came to them with power, the Holy Spirit, and full conviction (1 Thessalonians 1:5). The Holy Spirit gave them such a firm conviction that they were able to trust the message even when it resulted in persecution. The Spirit also works today to assure us of the truth of God's word. Bible study is much more than mastering the meaning of human words. It is embracing the story of Jesus through the power of the Spirit, even in the face of terror and trouble.

A Lived Spirituality

Spirituality can sometimes seem ethereal and otherworldly. Biblical spirituality is always practical, concerned with day by day obedience. Thus, Paul urges the Thessalonians to be sexually moral, because to live otherwise would be rejecting the Holy Spirit of God. He calls them (and us) to live as children of light—loving others, praying always, and working hard. To do otherwise would be extinguishing the Spirit's fire (1 Thessalonians 5:19).

A Spirituality of Anticipation

Although biblical spirituality is practical and this-worldly, it grows out of the full conviction that this world has been and will be transformed by Christ. Paul assures the Thessalonians that their loved ones who have died are merely sleeping, awaiting the call of Jesus to wake them to resurrected life. We live as children of light in this world eagerly anticipating the day when Jesus returns to take us with him. "And so we will be with the Lord forever" (1 Thessalonians 4:17). Spirituality is all about relationship with God, a relationship that lasts throughout eternity. First Thessalonians is the encouraging message of that loving, forever relationship.

MESSAGE AND MESSENGER

(I THESSALONIANS 1:1-2:12)

Day One Reading and Questions:

¹Paul, Silas and Timothy, To the church of the Thessalonians in God the Father and the Lord Jesus Christ: Grace and peace to you. ²We always thank God for all of you, mentioning you in our prayers. ³We continually remember before our God and Father your work produced by faith, your labor prompted by love, and your endurance inspired by hope in our Lord Jesus Christ. ⁴For we know, brothers loved by God, that he has chosen you, ⁵because our gospel came to you not simply with words, but also with power, with the Holy Spirit and with deep conviction. You know how we lived among you for your sake.

1) *What do faith, hope, and love produce in this passage? How do the gifts of God relate to our work for him?*

2) *What is the sign that the Thessalonians are chosen? How do we know God has chosen us?*

3) *Paul talks about the words he gave the Thessalonians but also about his way of living among them. What makes us trust a person's words?*

Day Two Reading and Questions:

⁶You became imitators of us and of the Lord; in spite of severe suffering, you welcomed the message with the joy given by the Holy Spirit. ⁷And so you became a model to all the believers in Macedonia and Achaia. ⁸The Lord's message rang out from you not only in Macedonia and Achaia—your faith in God has become known every-where. Therefore we do not need to say anything about it, ⁹for they themselves report what kind of reception you gave us. They tell how you turned to God from idols to serve the living and true God, ¹⁰and to wait for his Son from heaven, whom he raised from the dead—Jesus, who rescues us from the coming wrath.

1) *How are the Thessalonians a model to other believers? In what ways is your church a model church?*

2) *What idols have we turned from to follow God?*

3) *Is the Second Coming a day of wrath for Christians? Why not?*

Day Three Reading and Questions:

¹You know, brothers, that our visit to you was not a failure. ²We had previously suffered and been insulted in Philippi, as you know, but with the help of our God we dared to tell you his gospel in spite of strong opposition. ³For the appeal we make does not spring from error or impure motives, nor are we trying to trick you. ⁴On the contrary, we speak as men approved by God to be entrusted with the gospel. We are not trying to please men but God, who tests our hearts. ⁵You know we never used flattery, nor did we put on a mask to cover up

greed—God is our witness. [6]We were not looking for praise from men, not from you or anyone else.

    1) Are there religious teachers who try to trick others? How do we know they are tricking us?

    2) Shouldn't we try to please other people? What's the danger in being people-pleasers?

    3) What impure motives do false teachers have? What motives should a Christian teacher have?

DAY FOUR READING AND QUESTIONS:

As apostles of Christ we could have been a burden to you, [7]but we were gentle among you, like a mother caring for her little children. [8]We loved you so much that we were delighted to share with you not only the gospel of God but our lives as well, because you had become so dear to us. [9]Surely you remember, brothers, our toil and hardship; we worked night and day in order not to be a burden to anyone while we preached the gospel of God to you.

[10]You are witnesses, and so is God, of how holy, righteous and blameless we were among you who believed. [11]For you know that we dealt with each of you as a father deals with his own children, [12]encouraging, comforting and urging you to live lives worthy of God, who calls you into his kingdom and glory.

    1) What two family metaphors does Paul use for his behavior toward the Thessalonians?

    2) What does this say about the nature of genuine ministry?

3) *Who have been spiritual fathers and mothers to you? How did they treat you? Why does Paul spend so much time talking of his behavior toward the Thessalonians? Isn't it the message of the gospel that's important?*

DAY FIVE READING AND QUESTIONS:

Go back and read the entire passage.

1) *Will people accept the gospel from those who are harsh and manipulative?*

2) *Do we win more people to Christ through our words or our lives?*

3) *How should we treat those around us who are caught up in the idols of this age? How do we bring them good news?*

MEDITATION ON 1 THESSALONIANS 1:1-2:12

"The Lord's message rang out from you not only in Macedonia and Achaia—your faith in God has become known everywhere."

How do we ring out the message of the Lord everywhere in our time? Do we approach strangers on the street, asking, "How is your soul, today?" Do we ring out the message on radio, TV, and the Web? Do we make friends with others in order to convert them?

How did the Thessalonians ring out the message? The same way Paul had brought the message to them. Not just with his words, but with his life. He didn't manipulate them into faith. He didn't preach for money or fame. Instead, he treated them gently, like a mother or a father with an infant.

We can be model Christians like the Thessalonians only if our faith is lived, not merely spoken. Our lives must ring true with the message of Christ. We must be genuine and authentic in our relationship with others. This means we befriend them not to "convert" them, but because they are loved by God. We do not condemn but we nurture them—encouraging, comforting, and urging them to accept God's love.

Spreading the good news of Jesus is not something we do; it is something we are. The life of the messenger confirms the message. Paul knew that. The Thessalonians knew that. God knows that. That's why he did more than preach to creation. He became a part of it.

"Lord Jesus, live in us so we might bring your love to others. May that message of love ring true in our lives."

FIRM FAITH

(1 THESSALONIANS 2:13-3:13)

DAY ONE READING AND QUESTIONS:

[13]And we also thank God continually because, when you received the word of God, which you heard from us, you accepted it not as the word of men, but as it actually is, the word of God, which is at work in you who believe. [14]For you, brothers, became imitators of God's churches in Judea, which are in Christ Jesus: You suffered from your own countrymen the same things those churches suffered from the Jews, [15]who killed the Lord Jesus and the prophets and also drove us out. They displease God and are hostile to all men [16]in their effort to keep us from speaking to the Gentiles so that they may be saved. In this way they always heap up their sins to the limit. The wrath of God has come upon them at last.

1) In what way is the gospel the word of men? In what way is it the word of God?

2) How did this church imitate the churches in Judea? Are we called to the same kind of imitation?

3) Who was trying to keep Paul from speaking to the Gentiles? Why were they doing this? Give examples today of groups that some may think do not deserve the gospel.

Day Two Reading and Questions:

[17]But, brothers, when we were torn away from you for a short time (in person, not in thought), out of our intense longing we made every effort to see you. [18]For we wanted to come to you—certainly I, Paul, did, again and again—but Satan stopped us. [19]For what is our hope, our joy, or the crown in which we will glory in the presence of our Lord Jesus when he comes? Is it not you? [20]Indeed, you are our glory and joy.

[1]So when we could stand it no longer, we thought it best to be left by ourselves in Athens. [2]We sent Timothy, who is our brother and God's fellow worker in spreading the gospel of Christ, to strengthen and encourage you in your faith, [3]so that no one would be unsettled by these trials. You know quite well that we were destined for them. [4]In fact, when we were with you, we kept telling you that we would be persecuted. And it turned out that way, as you well know. [5]For this reason, when I could stand it no longer, I sent Timothy to find out about your faith. I was afraid that in some way the tempter might have tempted you and our efforts might have been useless.

1) *Paul states Satan stopped him. Do we see Satan at work stopping us from doing good? Give examples.*

2) *Paul calls them his hope, glory, joy, and crown. Name some people who are all that to you. Are you someone else's hope, glory, joy, and crown?*

3) *What does Paul fear more than he fears persecution? What does that say about his love for the Thessalonians?*

Day Three Reading and Questions:

[6]But Timothy has just now come to us from you and has brought good news about your faith and love. He has told us that you always have pleasant memories of us and that you long to see us, just as we also long to see you. [7]Therefore, brothers, in all our distress and persecution we were encouraged about you because of your faith. [8]For now we really live, since you are standing firm in the Lord. [9]How can we thank God enough for you in return for all the joy we have in the presence of our God because of you? [10]Night and day we pray most earnestly that we may see you again and supply what is lacking in your faith.

1) *What good news have you heard about the church lately? How did it make you feel?*

2) *Who do you thank God for? Who brings you joy in the presence of God?*

3) *How can Paul supply what is lacking in their faith? How do others supply what is lacking in ours?*

Day Four Reading and Questions:

[11]Now may our God and Father himself and our Lord Jesus clear the way for us to come to you. [12]May the Lord make your love increase and overflow for each other and for everyone else, just as ours does for you. [13]May he strengthen your hearts so that you will be blameless and holy in the presence of our God and Father when our Lord Jesus comes with all his holy ones.

1) *Earlier Paul had said that Satan had prevented his coming to the Thessalonians. Here he prays that God and Jesus will clear the way for him. Do we have as clear a sense that God is guiding our lives? Should we?*

2) *How can the Lord make our love increase? Don't we have to make the effort to love others?*

3) *Do we think of ourselves as blameless and holy? Should we? If so, what makes us that way?*

Day Five Reading and Questions:

Go back and read the entire passage:

1) *How did the Thessalonians show their faith in this passage? How do we show our faith today?*

2) *Why was Paul concerned that the Thessalonians had lost their faith? Is faith fragile? What threatens our faith today?*

3) *How are faith and love related in these verses? Can one have true faith without love? Love without faith?*

MEDITATION ON 1 THESSALONIANS 2:13-3:13

Is our faith fragile or firm?

If we are honest we must answer, "Both." So it was with the Thessalonians. When the good news came to them through Paul, they trusted the messenger and the message and received that news as the word of God. What faith that took! Particularly when accepting that message resulted in their persecution.

But then the messenger left. Paul is torn away from them. He wants to return but cannot.

That had to make the Thessalonians wonder. Did Paul not care for them? Had they been taken in by some fast-talking religious salesman? Was this message about Jesus too strange or too good to be true? Were they stupid to suffer persecution for their beliefs?

Faith is a fragile thing. For the Thessalonians. For us. Those same doubts creep into our own hearts. Do I believe simply because my parents told me to? Isn't the Christian story too strange or too wonderful to believe? Is it worth giving up the pleasures of my former life if I cannot be absolutely certain of the gospel?

But Paul finds that the Thessalonians faith is firm, not fragile. It is a trust strengthened by the fires of persecution. It is a faith that shows itself in love for Paul, for fellow Christians, for neighbors, and for enemies. It is a humble faith that knows it needs the strength of others like Paul.

Is our faith fragile? Then we must rely even more on the power of God. Is our faith lacking? Then we turn to faithful brothers and sisters for strength. Is the good news hard to believe? Then we focus on the center of that news, Jesus who is coming again.

"Lord Jesus, increase our faith! Strengthen our hearts. Grow our love."

ENCOURAGING WORDS

(1 THESSALONIANS 4:1-18)

DAY ONE READING AND QUESTIONS:

¹Finally, brothers, we instructed you how to live in order to please God, as in fact you are living. Now we ask you and urge you in the Lord Jesus to do this more and more. ²For you know what instructions we gave you by the authority of the Lord Jesus.

³It is God's will that you should be sanctified: that you should avoid sexual immorality; ⁴that each of you should learn to control his own body in a way that is holy and honorable, ⁵not in passionate lust like the heathen, who do not know God; ⁶and that in this matter no one should wrong his brother or take advantage of him. The Lord will punish men for all such sins, as we have already told you and warned you. ⁷For God did not call us to be impure, but to live a holy life. ⁸Therefore, he who rejects this instruction does not reject man but God, who gives you his Holy Spirit.

1) *Why does the Bible place so much emphasis on sexual morality? Are Christians to be puritanical or against sex? Are sexual sins worse than others?*

2) *How can one wrong a brother or take advantage of him through sexual sin? Is sex a private matter or does it affect others?*

3) *What is the relationship between the Holy Spirit and holy living? Between the Holy Spirit and sexual morality?*

Day Two Reading and Questions:

[9]Now about brotherly love we do not need to write to you, for you yourselves have been taught by God to love each other. [10]And in fact, you do love all the brothers throughout Macedonia. Yet we urge you, brothers, to do so more and more.

[11]Make it your ambition to lead a quiet life, to mind your own business and to work with your hands, just as we told you, [12]so that your daily life may win the respect of outsiders and so that you will not be dependent on anybody.

1) *Love each other more and more. Is this a cliché? How do we love each other more?*

2) *What comes to mind when you hear "ambition"? Is leading a quiet life ambitious? Does the description of ambition here redefine the word?*

3) *Shouldn't we as Christians depend on each other? What does it mean that we should not be dependent on anybody?*

Day Three Reading and Questions:

[13]Brothers, we do not want you to be ignorant about those who fall asleep, or to grieve like the rest of men, who have no hope. [14]We believe that Jesus died and rose again and so we believe that God will bring with Jesus those who have fallen asleep in him. [15]According to

the Lord's own word, we tell you that we who are still alive, who are left till the coming of the Lord, will certainly not precede those who have fallen asleep.

1) *Why does the Bible often refer to the dead as sleeping? What does this say about the Christian view of death?*

2) *Should Christians grieve? How is our grief different from others?*

3) *What is harder to believe, that Jesus rose from the dead or that those we love will rise? Why?*

Day Four Reading and Questions:

[16]For the Lord himself will come down from heaven, with a loud command, with the voice of the archangel and with the trumpet call of God, and the dead in Christ will rise first. [17]After that, we who are still alive and are left will be caught up together with them in the clouds to meet the Lord in the air. And so we will be with the Lord forever. [18]Therefore encourage each other with these words.

1) *What is the significance of the loud command, voice of the archangel, and trumpet call? Whose attention is Jesus trying to get?*

2) *Paul says, "We who are left alive...." Did Paul expect to be alive when Jesus returned? Was he? Should we expect Jesus to return in our lifetime?*

3) *Why are these encouraging words?*

Day Five Reading and Questions:

Go back and read the entire passage.

1) *What is the connection between living holy lives and waiting for the coming of Jesus?*

2) *What is the connection between living a quiet life and waiting for the coming of Jesus?*

3) *We don't know exactly what life after death is like and don't know completely what "being with the Lord forever" is like. Does this lack of knowledge make it hard to believe in the resurrection?*

MEDITATION ON 1 THESSALONIANS 4:1-18

Waiting. Waiting is always hard. It's hard to wait on the coming of Jesus. It's been two thousand years! It's hard to wait for the resurrection of our loved ones. Standing at the graveside, death seems so final. It's hard to wait for the eternal pleasures of being with the Lord, particularly when we must give up the pleasures of unrestrained sexuality. It's hard to resist the call to worldly ambition, but instead to live quiet lives of daily work.

But waiting is so much easier if it is anticipation. Waiting for Christmas as a child was hard but it was a different kind of waiting from waiting in the dentist's office. We wait for what is to come with joyful anticipation. Those whom we love so much—mother, father, wife, husband, child, friend—will be restored to us on the day Jesus returns. We will greet our returning King in the air and live with him forever in a new heaven and a new earth.

This great anticipation changes how we live now. Our waiting is not merely killing time, but is an active waiting. We wait in holiness brought by the Holy Spirit. We wait in love, not harming our brothers and sisters by breaking up their marriages and breaking their hearts by our sexual immorality. We wait quietly, doing our daily work diligently, knowing that we are serving the Lord who is returning for us.

It is hard to have that sense of anticipation after two thousand years. But that is our calling. Whether Jesus comes sooner or later, he is coming. That marvelous return changes our view of everything— sexuality, ambition, relationships, and even death. Each day we need to hear these encouraging words. Each day we need to tell them.

We and those we love will be with the Lord forever. Anticipation.

"God of love, our Father, we know you hold those faithful dead in your hand. Lord Jesus, come quickly! Holy Spirit, make us holy as we anticipate that coming."

LIVING IN LIGHT
(1 THESSALONIANS 5:1-28)

Day One Reading and Questions:

¹Now, brothers, about times and dates we do not need to write to you, ²for you know very well that the day of the Lord will come like a thief in the night. ³While people are saying, "Peace and safety," destruction will come on them suddenly, as labor pains on a pregnant woman, and they will not escape.

⁴But you, brothers, are not in darkness so that this day should surprise you like a thief. ⁵You are all sons of the light and sons of the day. We do not belong to the night or to the darkness. ⁶So then, let us not be like others, who are asleep, but let us be alert and self-controlled. ⁷For those who sleep, sleep at night, and those who get drunk, get drunk at night.

1) *We don't want thieves to come but we should want Jesus to come. What does it mean that he will come like a thief?*

2) *Will the second coming be a surprise to us? Should it be?*

3) *What does it mean here to be awake? What is the contrast between this wakefulness and what others do at night?*

Day Two Reading and Questions:

[8]But since we belong to the day, let us be self-controlled, putting on faith and love as a breastplate, and the hope of salvation as a helmet. [9]For God did not appoint us to suffer wrath but to receive salvation through our Lord Jesus Christ. [10]He died for us so that, whether we are awake or asleep, we may live together with him. [11]Therefore encourage one another and build each other up, just as in fact you are doing.

1) *What is the point of the armor language here? How does it relate to living in the day vs. the night?*

2) *Do you ever feel under the wrath of God? What does it mean that God did not appoint us to suffer wrath? Is punishment God's will for us?*

3) *What does "awake or asleep" mean here in light of the last chapter?*

Day Three Reading and Questions:

[12]Now we ask you, brothers, to respect those who work hard among you, who are over you in the Lord and who admonish you. [13]Hold them in the highest regard in love because of their work. Live in peace with each other. [14]And we urge you, brothers, warn those who are idle, encourage the timid, help the weak, be patient with everyone. [15]Make sure that nobody pays back wrong for wrong, but always try to be kind to each other and to everyone else.

[16]Be joyful always; [17]pray continually; [18]give thanks in all circumstances, for this is God's will for you in Christ Jesus.

¹⁹Do not put out the Spirit's fire; ²⁰do not treat prophecies with contempt. ²¹Test everything. Hold on to the good. ²²Avoid every kind of evil.

1) *There are so many commands here. What holds them together? What theme do you find in them all?*

2) *More than once this letter encourages hard work. Do works save us? If not, why should we work so hard?*

3) *What does it mean to put out the Spirit's fire? Give examples of how we sometimes quench the Spirit.*

DAY FOUR READING AND QUESTIONS:

²³May God himself, the God of peace, sanctify you through and through. May your whole spirit, soul and body be kept blameless at the coming of our Lord Jesus Christ. ²⁴The one who calls you is faithful and he will do it.

²⁵Brothers, pray for us. ²⁶Greet all the brothers with a holy kiss. ²⁷I charge you before the Lord to have this letter read to all the brothers.

²⁸The grace of our Lord Jesus Christ be with you.

1) *What does it mean to be sanctified? How have you experienced that in your own life?*

2) *What is the difference among spirit, soul, and body? Why does he include our bodies in this list of what God makes blameless?*

3) *Why is it important to say the Lord is faithful? How do we see his faithfulness in our lives?*

Day Five Reading and Questions:

Go back and read the entire passage.

1) *What is the significance of light and day in this passage? How do we live as children of light?*

2) *How should we treat our brothers and sisters according to this passage? Why should we warn some but encourage others.*

3) *What is the place of prayer in Christian living?*

MEDITATION ON 1 THESSALONIANS 5:1-28

I write this on a gloomy day, one of a long series of gloomy days. I long for the light.

Worse than gloomy days are troubled nights. We fear the darkness. Crime and violence leap out at us from dark corners. Pain intensifies at night. Our doubts and worries multiply during sleepless nights. We cannot wait until morning.

God is light. He is the light that gives heat in a cold existence. He is the light that shows us the path in which we walk. He is the dawn that banishes our pains and fears. He asks us to walk in his light.

What does it mean to be children of the light? It means we wait patiently for the night to end with the dawning of Christ's return. It means we control ourselves, respect our leaders, warn the lazy, and encourage the weak. To walk in light means we must bring God's light to others.

What does it mean to be children of light? It means we trust the Father of light. We pray to him in confidence, thankfulness, and joy.

We open ourselves to his Spirit. We let him sanctify us through and through.

This is a dark world. All one has to do is to watch the news or read the papers to feel the weight of the darkness that surrounds us. God has shown his light into our world. Let us live as children of light, trusting that God is at work among us, that Jesus will soon return, that the Spirit is making us holy. God is faithful. Let us live in his light.

"God of light, shine into our hearts so we may live your light before others. In a world of darkness may we hold on to all that is good."

2 THESSALONIANS: JESUS IS COMING

THE SPIRITUALITY OF 2 THESSALONIANS

In this brief letter we find a spirituality that touches on some of the most profound teachings of Scripture—justice, salvation and sanctification. At the same time, it is a daily, this-worldly spirituality that shapes the workplace.

A Spirituality of Justice

In our time, many equate a God of grace and love with a God who is "soft" on evil. But graciously forging sin is not the same as ignoring deceit and violence. The Thessalonians are suffering unjustly for their faith, but they suffer in the hope that God will bring justice. God wants to save all but he will not save them in their rebellion. There is lawlessness and rebellion against God now, but the day will come when Jesus returns to destroy the lawless. To be truly spiritual means to hunger for justice and to work for it now while we trust God alone to bring ultimate vindication and justice.

A Sanctifying, Saving Spirituality

Some Christians make a strong division between justification (being saved from sin) and sanctification (being made holy by God), even calling these two separate works of grace. Paul here speaks of being "saved through the sanctifying work of the Spirit" (2 Thessalonians 2:13). Being spiritual or sanctified is not something added to our salvation. It is not optional for those already saved but is the actual process of salvation. God is saving us through his Spirit who works his will within us.

A Spirituality of Work

If Jesus is coming again to put things right, if salvation is by grace from beginning to end, if God gives us daily bread, then why work? All of these teachings are true but should not lead to idleness. Paul himself is a model of work. One must work to eat. One who is not busy easily becomes a busybody. This is not mere realistic economics, but a call to make all our work for God, to never tire of doing right because it is the Spirit who works in us.

MEDITATIONS ON 2 THESSALONIANS:

GOD IS JUST

(2 THESSALONIANS 1:1-2:12)

DAY ONE READING AND QUESTIONS:

¹Paul, Silas and Timothy,

To the church of the Thessalonians in God our Father and the Lord Jesus Christ:

²Grace and peace to you from God the Father and the Lord Jesus Christ.

³We ought always to thank God for you, brothers, and rightly so, because your faith is growing more and more, and the love every one of you has for each other is increasing. ⁴Therefore, among God's churches we boast about your perseverance and faith in all the persecutions and trials you are enduring.

⁵All this is evidence that God's judgment is right, and as a result you will be counted worthy of the kingdom of God, for which you are suffering.

1) *How does a church show that its faith and love are increasing?*

2) *Do you boast about your church? What do you boast about?*

3) *How does the growth of the Thessalonians prove that God's judgment is right? What does "judgment" mean here?*

Day Two Reading and Questions:

[6]God is just: He will pay back trouble to those who trouble you [7]and give relief to you who are troubled, and to us as well. This will happen when the Lord Jesus is revealed from heaven in blazing fire with his powerful angels. [8]He will punish those who do not know God and do not obey the gospel of our Lord Jesus. [9]They will be punished with everlasting destruction and shut out from the presence of the Lord and from the majesty of his power [10]on the day he comes to be glorified in his holy people and to be marveled at among all those who have believed. This includes you, because you believed our testimony to you.

[11]With this in mind, we constantly pray for you, that our God may count you worthy of his calling, and that by his power he may fulfill every good purpose of yours and every act prompted by your faith. [12]We pray this so that the name of our Lord Jesus may be glorified in you, and you in him, according to the grace of our God and the Lord Jesus Christ.

1) *Should we want God to pay back those who trouble us? Shouldn't we forgive our enemies?*

2) *How are we to be worthy of the calling of God? Aren't we saved by grace? Are we not all unworthy?*

3) *What is God's part in our good purposes and acts? What is our part?*

Day Three Reading and Questions:

[1]Concerning the coming of our Lord Jesus Christ and our being gathered to him, we ask you, brothers, [2]not to become easily unsettled

or alarmed by some prophecy, report or letter supposed to have come from us, saying that the day of the Lord has already come. ³Don't let anyone deceive you in any way, for that day will not come until the rebellion occurs and the man of lawlessness is revealed, the man doomed to destruction. ⁴He will oppose and will exalt himself over everything that is called God or is worshiped, so that he sets himself up in God's temple, proclaiming himself to be God.

1) *Why would anyone think the Lord had already come? Are there those today that think this? Can we miss the Second Coming?*

2) *It seems that some were writing fake letters in the name of Paul. Do some today claim to speak for Paul? For Jesus? How should we regard such claims?*

3) *No one seems to know for certain who "the man of lawlessness" is. Name some historical or contemporary people that resemble the description of the man of lawlessness.*

Day Four Reading and Questions:

⁵Don't you remember that when I was with you I used to tell you these things? ⁶And now you know what is holding him back, so that he may be revealed at the proper time. ⁷For the secret power of lawlessness is already at work; but the one who now holds it back will continue to do so till he is taken out of the way. ⁸And then the lawless one will be revealed, whom the Lord Jesus will overthrow with the breath of his mouth and destroy by the splendor of his coming. ⁹The coming of the lawless one will be in accordance with the work of Satan displayed in all kinds of counterfeit miracles, signs and wonders, ¹⁰and in every sort of evil that deceives those who are

perishing. They perish because they refused to love the truth and so be saved. [11]For this reason God sends them a powerful delusion so that they will believe the lie [12]and so that all will be condemned who have not believed the truth but have delighted in wickedness.

1) *Who is holding back the man of lawlessness? Why is he holding him back?*

2) *Who will destroy the lawless one? How?*

3) *Why would God send some a powerful delusion? Does God allow us to be self-deceived? How do we keep ourselves from deception?*

DAY FIVE READING AND QUESTIONS:

Go back and read the entire passage:

1) *Should we be afraid of the man of lawlessness? How should we react to him? Do you tend to be overly aware of false teachers or tend to believe there are no false teachers? Why?*

2) *What will Jesus do when he comes again, according to this passage? Does that make you anticipate the coming of Jesus more or anticipate it less?*

3) *If God is love, why does he so often condemn?*

MEDITATION ON 2 THESSALONIANS 1:1-2:12

"The man of lawlessness." He sounds like such a shadowy figure, almost like the bad guy in the superhero movies. Perhaps for that reason we might quickly dismiss him as a real threat.

On the other hand, some Christians like to scare themselves and others with lurid pictures of the world ruled by the antichrist. They live in constant fear of the latest lunatic dictator, imagining that the great Tribulation has come.

So what should we do, ignore this warning of the man of lawlessness or cower in fear of him? The answer is neither. Paul wants us to take evil seriously. There are false teachers and deceivers in the world. We must not be so naïve as to think they pose no danger to us. We must be aware and on our guard. We must not be taken in.

But this is not a call to paranoia. When others claim to be faithful Christians, we should accept them as such. The golden rule calls us to this. We want them to trust us, so we trust them. However, if by their actions (their "fruits" as Jesus says) they prove to be self-serving deceivers, then we must watch out for them.

Who is the man of lawlessness? Has he already come? Is he still to come? I don't know. What we do know is that many deceivers are in the world. What's more, we know that Jesus is more powerful than any deceiver, even Satan, the great deceiver. The Lord Jesus will overthrow the man of lawlessness and will utterly defeat Satan. Good will triumph. Evil will fall.

So we must not be deceived, but we must not live in fear. Although it might look as though evil is winning, the Lord we serve is all-powerful. He will give us triumph over the evils of today and will protect us from the evils of tomorrow. He will bring justice, punishing evil and rewarding the faithful. God is in control. No one can successfully rebel against him.

"Father, give us confidence in your power and love. Remove our fear. Open our eyes to deception. Keep us faithful in hardship."

PRAY AND WORK

(2 THESSALONIANS 2:13-3:18)

Day One Reading and Questions:

[13]But we ought always to thank God for you, brothers loved by the Lord, because from the beginning God chose you to be saved through the sanctifying work of the Spirit and through belief in the truth. [14]He called you to this through our gospel, that you might share in the glory of our Lord Jesus Christ. [15]So then, brothers, stand firm and hold to the teachings we passed on to you, whether by word of mouth or by letter.

[16]May our Lord Jesus Christ himself and God our Father, who loved us and by his grace gave us eternal encouragement and good hope, [17]encourage your hearts and strengthen you in every good deed and word.

1) *We are saved by the sanctifying work of the Spirit. How does being made holy (sanctified) save us? Is there a difference between salvation and sanctification?*

2) *How did God choose us? How did he call us? How should we respond to that choice and that call?*

3) *Paul says to hold to the teachings (literally, "traditions") he had passed on to them. How is tradition a positive word? Can tradition be a negative word? How?*

Day Two Reading and Questions:

[1]Finally, brothers, pray for us that the message of the Lord may spread rapidly and be honored, just as it was with you. [2]And pray that we may be delivered from wicked and evil men, for not everyone has faith. [3]But the Lord is faithful, and he will strengthen and protect you from the evil one. [4]We have confidence in the Lord that you are doing and will continue to do the things we command. [5]May the Lord direct your hearts into God's love and Christ's perseverance.

1) *What does Paul request in prayer? What should we request?*

2) *Why is it important to know that the Lord is faithful? How does he show his faithfulness? How should we respond to his faithfulness?*

3) *How did Christ persevere? How do our hearts share in his perseverance?*

Day Three Reading and Questions:

[6]In the name of the Lord Jesus Christ, we command you, brothers, to keep away from every brother who is idle and does not live according to the teaching you received from us. [7]For you yourselves know how you ought to follow our example. We were not idle when we were with you, [8]nor did we eat anyone's food without paying for it. On the contrary, we worked night and day, laboring and toiling so that we would not be a burden to any of you. [9]We did this, not because we do not have the right to such help, but in order to make ourselves a model for you to follow. [10]For even when we were with you, we gave you this rule: "If a man will not work, he shall not eat."

[11]We hear that some among you are idle. They are not busy; they are busybodies. [12]Such people we command and urge in the Lord Jesus Christ to settle down and earn the bread they eat. [13]And as for you, brothers, never tire of doing what is right.

1) *"If a man will not work, he shall not eat." Is this a harsh rule? Should we use this as an excuse for not helping the poor? Could most poor people find jobs if they wanted to?*

2) *What is a busybody? Are some that way because they have too much time on their hands?*

3) *Can we be too busy? Is that as bad as not being busy enough? If we are too busy, might that make us tired of doing what is right?*

Day Four Reading and Questions:

[14]If anyone does not obey our instruction in this letter, take special note of him. Do not associate with him, in order that he may feel ashamed. [15]Yet do not regard him as an enemy, but warn him as a brother. [16]Now may the Lord of peace himself give you peace at all times and in every way. The Lord be with all of you.

[17]I, Paul, write this greeting in my own hand, which is the distinguishing mark in all my letters. This is how I write. [18]The grace of our Lord Jesus Christ be with you all.

1) *How can we make people ashamed and still treat them as brothers and sisters?*

2) *Do we sometimes try to keep peace in the church by avoiding confrontation? Should we? How can we confront and still follow the Lord of peace?*

3) *In light of what he said earlier, why is it important that Paul signs his letters?*

Day Five Reading and Questions:

Go back and read the entire passage.

1) *Why is it important that we work? Should we get our identity or worth from our work?*

2) *If we are saved by grace, what is the place of good deeds in our salvation?*

3) *Is shame good or bad?*

MEDITATION ON 2 THESSALONIANS 2:13-3:18

Work. Perhaps, like me you've always had mixed feelings about work. Sometimes work is satisfying, refreshing both body and soul. At other times it borders on toil—mind numbing, backbreaking work.

God made work for human beings from the beginning. Adam and Eve worked in the garden even before they sinned. But after sin entered the world, God cursed the ground and cursed humanity with more difficult work.

We can work too little. Some in Thessalonica were refusing to work. Paul reminds us that God expects us to work to provide for ourselves, our families, and those in need.

We also can make work too important. When we meet new people we usually ask them, "And what do you do?" We would be surprised if they answered, "Oh, I sleep and eat and read and play."

What we want to know is their occupation. Our jobs give us identity, "I'm a teacher, lawyer, bricklayer, nurse, or plumber." But we are much more than what we do for a living. We are children of God.

If we are confused about work, we are more confused about works. I grew up singing many "work" hymns—"To the Work," "Work, Work for Jesus," "Work, For the Night is Coming." We were a working church! So much so that we sometimes forgot the grace of God.

We are saved by grace. By his grace and through his Spirit, God is at work among us and in us. We work by his power through prayer. That's why Paul wants the Thessalonians to pray for him. That's why he says earlier in this letter, "With this in mind, we constantly pray for you, that our God may count you worthy of his calling, and that by his power he may fulfill every good purpose of yours and every act prompted by your faith" (2 Thessalonians 1:11)

Prayer and work. They always go together.

"Father, work your will in us today through your Holy Spirit."

1 TIMOTHY: JESUS TRAINS US

THE SPIRITUALITY OF 1 TIMOTHY

This looks like a personal letter Paul writes to Timothy, his true child in the faith. In many ways, it is personal. Yet it gives advice on ministry and church life that Christians through the ages need to hear. Although the letter rarely mentions the Holy Spirit, he is there guiding the instruction Paul gives to Timothy and to us about how to live out the faith in these difficult latter times. He is the one who trains us in godliness.

THE SPIRIT AND CONTROVERSY

Several times Paul warns Timothy that controversies, anger, disputes, and arguments over words come from false teachers who do not live the truth. Those who foster controversy in order to gain power have sidetracked many a healthy, spiritual church. Although they appear to be fighters for the faith, they do not promote the work of God, which is love.

PRAYING AND HOLINESS

Instead of arguing, God's people are to pray. We make our requests to God. We intercede for others in need. We pray in thankfulness for all God has given us. We particularly pray for rulers so that we, as God's people, may "live peaceful and quiet lives in all godliness and holiness" (1 Timothy 2:2). We pray not just to get things from God but to be closer to him. Our greatest request is that he will shape us through his Spirit into godly, holy people.

LEADERSHIP AND MYSTERY

Paul gives advice to leaders. Whether elders, deacons, older women, or Timothy himself, all are to live out the mystery of godliness. That mystery centers on the story of Jesus who died and was raised for us (1 Timothy 3:16). We fight the good fight of faith and encourage others to do so by both our teaching and our lives. (1 Timothy 4:16).

GODLINESS OR MONEY

One great danger to a healthy faith is the desire for riches. Those who are rich should not be arrogant or hope in riches but should share with others generously (1 Timothy 6:17-18). Not just the rich but those who desire to be rich fall into many temptations and traps (1 Timothy 6:9-10). Most dangerous of all are those who lead others astray for financial gain. True treasure is in godliness, not money

MEDITATIONS ON 1 THIMOTHY:

UNLIMITED PATIENCE

(1 TIMOTHY 1:1-20)

Day One Reading and Questions:

¹Paul, an apostle of Christ Jesus by the command of God our Savior and of Christ Jesus our hope,

²To Timothy my true son in the faith:

Grace, mercy and peace from God the Father and Christ Jesus our Lord.

³As I urged you when I went into Macedonia, stay there in Ephesus so that you may command certain men not to teach false doctrines any longer ⁴nor to devote themselves to myths and endless genealogies. These promote controversies rather than God's work— which is by faith.

1) Who are some of your fathers and mothers in the faith? Who are your sons and daughters in the faith? How do we feel toward these people?

2) How do you react to the term, "false doctrine"? What are some false teachings about Christianity in our world today?

3) Do controversies ever promote the work of God?

Day Two Reading and Questions:

[5]The goal of this command is love, which comes from a pure heart and a good conscience and a sincere faith. [6]Some have wandered away from these and turned to meaningless talk. [7]They want to be teachers of the law, but they do not know what they are talking about or what they so confidently affirm.

[8]We know that the law is good if one uses it properly. [9]We also know that law is made not for the righteous but for lawbreakers and rebels, the ungodly and sinful, the unholy and irreligious; for those who kill their fathers or mothers, for murderers, [10]for adulterers and perverts, for slave traders and liars and perjurers—and for whatever else is contrary to the sound doctrine [11]that conforms to the glorious gospel of the blessed God, which he entrusted to me.

1) *Give some contemporary examples of confident but meaningless talk in the name of Jesus. What should we do about such teachers?*

2) *Are you surprised that Paul says the law is good? How is it good?*

3) *What is the purpose of the law according to this passage? What place should law have in the life of Christians?*

Day Three Reading and Questions:

[12]I thank Christ Jesus our Lord, who has given me strength, that he considered me faithful, appointing me to his service. [13]Even though I was once a blasphemer and a persecutor and a violent man, I was shown mercy because I acted in ignorance and unbelief. [14]The grace of our Lord was poured out on me abundantly, along with the faith and love that are in Christ Jesus.

¹⁵Here is a trustworthy saying that deserves full acceptance: Christ Jesus came into the world to save sinners—of whom I am the worst. ¹⁶But for that very reason I was shown mercy so that in me, the worst of sinners, Christ Jesus might display his unlimited patience as an example for those who would believe on him and receive eternal life. ¹⁷Now to the King eternal, immortal, invisible, the only God, be honor and glory for ever and ever. Amen.

1) *Why did God show mercy to Paul?*

2) *Was Paul the worst of sinners? Why were his sins the worst?*

3) *Why do you think Paul breaks out into praise for God in this passage?*

Day Four Reading and Questions:

¹⁸Timothy, my son, I give you this instruction in keeping with the prophecies once made about you, so that by following them you may fight the good fight, ¹⁹holding on to faith and a good conscience. Some have rejected these and so have shipwrecked their faith. ²⁰Among them are Hymenaeus and Alexander, whom I have handed over to Satan to be taught not to blaspheme.

1) *What prophecies do you think were made about Timothy? Is this referring to Old Testament prophecies?*

2) *What is the good fight? How does one fight it?*

3) *What does it mean to hand one over to Satan? Is this a loving thing to do?*

Day Five Reading and Questions:

Go back and read the entire passage.

1) *Why does Paul receive mercy as the chief of sinners while Hymenaeus and Alexander are delivered over to Satan? Does Jesus play favorites?*

2) *Jesus has unlimited patience. Does this mean he will forgive everyone their sins? Will everyone be saved?*

3) *If salvation is by grace and mercy, how is it like a fight? What are we fighting for? Against? How should we fight?*

MEDITATION ON 1 TIMOTHY 1:1-20

Unlimited patience. That's what Jesus showed toward Paul, forgiving him even when he was the chief of sinners.

Unlimited patience. That's what we need from God and from others. That's what we must show to others.

But surely, patience has its limits. We must respect God's law. Those who break his law deserve punishment. False teachers must be silenced. Evil punished.

Yes, indeed. But God placed that punishment on Jesus. That same Jesus shows unlimited patience to Paul and to us.

But patience does not mean permission. Forgiveness is not approval. We can even reject the patience and forgiveness of Jesus by wrecking our faith, as did Hymenaeus and Alexander. But even then, they are delivered to Satan in order to move them toward repentance. It is to teach them not to blaspheme. No matter how intentionally we reject the grace of God through Jesus, he is patiently waiting for our return.

Patience is what we must show to others. Sometimes, it is a tough patience that teaches difficult lessons to our brothers and sisters. But even then, the goal is not to enforce the law. The goal is not to win the controversy, or stamp out false teaching, or even to fight the good fight. The goal is love.

"Lord Jesus, thank you for being infinitely patient with us. Thank you for teaching us even the painful, difficult lessons. Give us patience toward others."

MEN AND WOMEN PRAY

(2 TIMOTHY 2:1-15)

DAY ONE READING AND QUESTIONS:

¹I urge, then, first of all, that requests, prayers, intercession and thanksgiving be made for everyone— ²for kings and all those in authority, that we may live peaceful and quiet lives in all godliness and holiness.

1) *Having just delivered Hymenaeus and Alexander to Satan, Paul now says to pray for everyone. Does this include Hymenaeus and Alexander? How should we pray for people like them?*

2) *We are to pray for all kings and those in authority. Does this include unjust rulers? Tyrants? Candidates we did not vote for? How do we pray for them all?*

3) *Should we pray that rulers should promote Christian values or that we should be permitted to live quiet and peaceful lives? What is the difference?*

DAY TWO READING AND QUESTIONS:

³This is good, and pleases God our Savior, ⁴who wants all men to be saved and to come to a knowledge of the truth. ⁵For there is one God and one mediator between God and men, the man Christ Jesus, ⁶who gave himself as a ransom for all men—the testimony given in its

proper time. [7]And for this purpose I was appointed a herald and an apostle—I am telling the truth, I am not lying—and a teacher of the true faith to the Gentiles.

1) If God wants all to be saved, will everyone be saved? Can we go against the will of God?

2) There is one mediator. Is Christianity a narrow, exclusive, and violent because Christians believe Jesus is the only mediator?

3) In what sense was the testimony about Jesus given at the proper time?

Day Three Reading and Questions:

[8]I want men everywhere to lift up holy hands in prayer, without anger or disputing.

[9]I also want women to dress modestly, with decency and propriety, not with braided hair or gold or pearls or expensive clothes, [10]but with good deeds, appropriate for women who profess to worship God.

1) Is there an intentional contrast between "holy hands" and anger or disputing? Are men more prone than women toward anger and disputing?

2) Is there a connection between modesty and prayer?

3) Is the description of modesty here more concerned with the amount of skin women show or their display of wealth?

DAY FOUR READING AND QUESTIONS:

[11]A woman should learn in quietness and full submission. [12]I do not permit a woman to teach or to have authority over a man; she must be silent. [13]For Adam was formed first, then Eve. [14]And Adam was not the one deceived; it was the woman who was deceived and became a sinner. [15]But women will be saved through childbearing—if they continue in faith, love and holiness with propriety.

1) *Are these instructions to women of every culture or only for Paul's day?*

2) *What is the point of Eve being created second and being deceived? Are women second-class? Are they more easily deceived than men?*

3) *What does it mean that women will be saved through childbearing?*

DAY FIVE READING AND QUESTIONS:

Go back and read the entire passage.

1) *Do men and women pray differently? If so, how?*

2) *Do men and women have different temptations—men prone to anger and women to immodesty?*

3) *Is this section primarily about the differences between men and women or about prayer?*

MEDITATION ON 1 TIMOTHY 2:1-15

Does this passage make us angry? Doesn't it go against our cherished views of the equality of men and women? Doesn't it put women down? They should be silent. They were made second. They were easily deceived. They might be saved if they have enough children.

Does Paul mean to offend? Is he against women? Is this the same writer who said, "There is neither Jew nor Greek, slave nor free, male nor female, for you are all one in Christ Jesus" (Galatians 3:28)"?

I'm not sure what to make of this passage. There are differences between men and women, some biological, some cultural. I don't believe the cultural differences between men and women in Paul's day were meant for all time.

What I am sure of is that this passage is more about prayer and living than it is about the proper role of men and women. How do we pray? We make "supplications," heartfelt requests to God for help through personal difficulty. "Prayers" also implies requests from God, but in a broader sense of asking for his care in all circumstances. "Intercessions" are prayers in behalf of our brothers, sisters, and neighbors. "Thanksgivings" spring naturally from our gratitude for God's gifts. These terms do not so much describe four separate types of prayer, but point to elements found in most prayers.

We pray these prayers for everyone, but particularly for kings and those in high position. In Paul's day, many rulers persecuted Christians, yet they are told to pray even for unjust rulers in hope that God will make the bad kings leave Christians in peace. Our God is so powerful he can work through evil rulers to accomplish his purposes. No matter what kind of government rules us, we still pray the authorities will allow us quiet and peaceable Christian lives.

As far as how to pray, we should lift up holy hands. The Bible gives many positions for prayer: standing, kneeling, bowing the face to the ground, lifting hands, and others. No one position is the only proper way of praying. What we must not do is belittle a brother or sister who prays in a different position. Prayer must be without anger or argument. Neither should we adopt an unusual prayer position to call attention to ourselves. Prayer is a time for Christians to unite in their petitions to God. It is not a time (indeed, there is never an acceptable time) for us to bicker and argue over how we pray.

Whatever our posture, something special happens when the church prays together. In a world where everyone looks out for number one, Christians put aside their differences and join together to approach their Father and encourage each other. What could be more beautiful than men and women praying?

"God our Savior, thank you for the privilege of prayer. May we always pour out our hearts to you, knowing that you want all to be saved."

LEADERS AND SERVANTS
(1 TIMOTHY 3:1-13)

DAY ONE READING AND QUESTIONS:

¹Here is a trustworthy saying: If anyone sets his heart on being an overseer, he desires a noble task. ²Now the overseer must be above reproach, the husband of but one wife, temperate, self-controlled, respectable, hospitable, able to teach, ³not given to drunkenness, not violent but gentle, not quarrelsome, not a lover of money.

> 1) *What do you think of when you hear the word "overseer"? What about "bishop" (other translations use this word)? Are there better words to describe Christian leaders?*

> 2) *Does "above reproach" mean no one criticizes you? Did people criticize Jesus? Was he above reproach?*

> 3) *Name various ways that church leaders teach.*

DAY TWO READING AND QUESTIONS:

⁴He must manage his own family well and see that his children obey him with proper respect. ⁵(If anyone does not know how to manage his own family, how can he take care of God's church?) ⁶He must not be a recent convert, or he may become conceited and fall

under the same judgment as the devil. [7]He must also have a good reputation with outsiders, so that he will not fall into disgrace and into the devil's trap.

1) Why is a church leader's home life important?

2) Why are gentleness and non-violence important in a church leader?

3) Is pride a danger for church leaders? Why?

Day Three Reading and Questions:

[8]Deacons, likewise, are to be men worthy of respect, sincere, not indulging in much wine, and not pursuing dishonest gain. [9]They must keep hold of the deep truths of the faith with a clear conscience. [10]They must first be tested; and then if there is nothing against them, let them serve as deacons.

1) What is the job of deacons in the church?

2) The "deep truths of the faith" is literally "the mystery." What is the mystery of the faith? Why describe it that way?

3) Why is it important to test or examine potential church leaders before we place them in leadership positions?

Day Four Reading and Questions:

[11]In the same way, their wives are to be women worthy of respect, not malicious talkers but temperate and trustworthy in everything.
[12]A deacon must be the husband of but one wife and must manage his children and his household well. [13]Those who have served well gain

an excellent standing and great assurance in their faith in Christ Jesus.

1) Literally, verse 11 addresses "women." Are these women deacons or wives of deacons? What makes you think so?

2) Why would slander undercut a leader's effectiveness?

3) What are the rewards of being a deacon?

Day Five Reading and Questions:

Go back and read the entire passage.

1) What are some good ways and some bad ways to choose church leaders?

2) Why would anyone want to be a church leader? What are some bad motivations for leadership?

3) How does good leadership protect churches from false teaching?

MEDITATION ON 1 TIMOTHY 3:1-13

What should we make of this familiar list of the qualifications for elders and deacons? In my experience, what we have done is combine it with a similar (but not identical) "list" from Titus 2:6-9, then argue about the meaning of some of the items (Does husband of one wife exclude the divorced? The widowed? Does "children" mean more than one child? Does believing children mean they must be baptized?), while ignoring the true purpose of these texts.

What is that purpose? To describe the character of Christian leaders who encourage others in healthy teaching. It is not a legalistic list (if so, why the differences between Timothy and Titus) but more like a job description.

As elders (or overseers) and deacons, it would be healthy to constantly refocus on the character traits described here and on the purpose of elders, that is to teach. Elders must embody their teaching. We teach what we live. We do not ask the flock to do anything the shepherd is not already doing. That's why these character descriptions are so important.

Healthy teaching comes not only from elders but also from others, including women. Why do I believe in God? Many reasons, but it really all boils down to this: my faith depends on the lives of godly women— my grandmother and mother—who passed the faith down to me. Not only older women but also older men embodied the good news of Jesus for me. In this I am not alone. All of us owe our faith to those who loved us enough to teach us the deep truths of the faith.

How can we have healthy churches? Good leaders. Good followers. Healthy teaching. Teaching as Jesus taught, by making disciples. Healthy teaching is holding the deep truths of the faith with a clear conscience. It is calling others to faith.

"Father, thank you for those who have led us in the faith. Give us love and respect for our leaders. May we lead others to you by our words and our lives."

TRAINING IN GODLINESS

(1 TIMOTHY 3:14-4:16)

DAY ONE READING AND QUESTIONS:

[14]Although I hope to come to you soon, I am writing you these instructions so that, [15]if I am delayed, you will know how people ought to conduct themselves in God's household, which is the church of the living God, the pillar and foundation of the truth. [16]Beyond all question, the mystery of godliness is great:

He appeared in a body,
　　was vindicated by the Spirit,
was seen by angels,
　　was preached among the nations,
was believed on in the world,
　　was taken up in glory.

1) *How is the church like a household or family?*

2) *Isn't truth the foundation of the church? Them how is the church the pillar and foundation of the truth?*

3) *What is the great mystery of godliness?*

DAY TWO READING AND QUESTIONS:

[1]The Spirit clearly says that in later times some will abandon the faith and follow deceiving spirits and things taught by demons. [2]Such teachings come through hypocritical liars, whose consciences have been seared as with a hot iron. [3]They forbid people to marry and order them to abstain from certain foods, which God created to be received with thanksgiving by those who believe and who know the truth. [4]For everything God created is good, and nothing is to be rejected if it is received with thanksgiving, [5]because it is consecrated by the word of God and prayer.

1) False teachers also live falsely. How do these verses describe them?

2) What do these false teachers teach against? Why would anyone follow these false teachings? Do you think they sound like strict religion to some?

3) Is everything God created good? Why don't we act that way sometimes?

DAY THREE READING AND QUESTIONS:

[6]If you point these things out to the brothers, you will be a good minister of Christ Jesus, brought up in the truths of the faith and of the good teaching that you have followed. [7]Have nothing to do with godless myths and old wives' tales; rather, train yourself to be godly. [8]For physical training is of some value, but godliness has value for all things, holding promise for both the present life and the life to come.
[9]This is a trustworthy saying that deserves full acceptance [10](and for this we labor and strive), that we have put our hope in the living God, who is the Savior of all men, and especially of those who believe.

1) What are some things we waste time arguing about in church? Do those arguments bring us closer to God?

2) What is the difference between trying to be godly and training in godliness? Can we do more through training or through trying harder?

3) How does hope help us as we labor and strive?

Day Four Reading and Questions:

[11]Command and teach these things. [12]Don't let anyone look down on you because you are young, but set an example for the believers in speech, in life, in love, in faith and in purity. [13]Until I come, devote yourself to the public reading of Scripture, to preaching and to teaching. [14]Do not neglect your gift, which was given you through a prophetic message when the body of elders laid their hands on you.

[15]Be diligent in these matters; give yourself wholly to them, so that everyone may see your progress. [16]Watch your life and doctrine closely. Persevere in them, because if you do, you will save both yourself and your hearers.

1) Are there those in the church we look down upon because they are young? Why do we do that? Should we?

2) Does your church emphasize the reading of Scripture? How can we better promote Bible reading?

3) Why is it important for Timothy to pay attention to his life as well as his teachings?

DAY FIVE READING AND QUESTIONS:

Go back and read the entire passage.

1) *What is the true faith that the false teachers have abandoned? Is this the same as the mystery of faith mentioned in this passage?*

2) *What is the relationship between true and false teaching and true and false living? Can we teach the truth without living it?*

3) *What does the Holy Spirit do in this passage?*

MEDITATION ON 1 TIMOTHY 3:14-4:16

We can do much more through training than through trying.

Whether it's hitting a baseball, waterskiing, or running a marathon, none of us could do these things the first time we tried. It took practice, instruction, repetition, and discipline to learn these skills.

So also with our spiritual lives. We must train ourselves to be godly. Such training requires practice, instruction, repetition, and discipline. We train by praying, reading Scripture, being thankful, and by being examples in speech, life, love, faith, and purity.

Training sounds like hard work. It is! But we know good works do not save us. Training is the way we embrace the gift God has given us instead of neglecting that gift. Training does not make God love us but it opens our hearts and lives to receive his love.

Such training also makes us able to discern true and healthy teaching from false, demonic doctrine. Training also strengthens our hope in the great mystery of godliness, the mystery of a Savior who took on a body, overcame death, was proclaimed to the nations, and now lives in glory. These are more than mere words or doctrines to us. They are the truths we live out in this mystery we call life.

"Father, we thank you for revealing the mystery of Jesus to us. Train us to be godly so we can accept your gifts with joy."

OLDER AND YOUNGER

(1 TIMOTHY 5:1-6:2)

DAY ONE READING AND QUESTIONS:

¹Do not rebuke an older man harshly, but exhort him as if he were your father. Treat younger men as brothers, ²older women as mothers, and younger women as sisters, with absolute purity. ³Give proper recognition to those widows who are really in need. ⁴But if a widow has children or grandchildren, these should learn first of all to put their religion into practice by caring for their own family and so repaying their parents and grandparents, for this is pleasing to God. ⁵The widow who is really in need and left all alone puts her hope in God and continues night and day to pray and to ask God for help. ⁶But the widow who lives for pleasure is dead even while she lives. ⁷Give the people these instructions, too, so that no one may be open to blame. ⁸If anyone does not provide for his relatives, and especially for his immediate family, he has denied the faith and is worse than an unbeliever.

1) *Should we treat people differently based on their gender and age? Why?*

2) *What is our responsibility toward aging parents and grandparents?*

3) *Some widows live for God, some for themselves. Is this true only of widows?*

Day Two Reading and Questions:

[9]No widow may be put on the list of widows unless she is over sixty, has been faithful to her husband, [10]and is well known for her good deeds, such as bringing up children, showing hospitality, washing the feet of the saints, helping those in trouble and devoting herself to all kinds of good deeds.

[11]As for younger widows, do not put them on such a list. For when their sensual desires overcome their dedication to Christ, they want to marry. [12]Thus they bring judgment on themselves, because they have broken their first pledge. [13]Besides, they get into the habit of being idle and going about from house to house. And not only do they become idlers, but also gossips and busybodies, saying things they ought not to. [14]So I counsel younger widows to marry, to have children, to manage their homes and to give the enemy no opportunity for slander. [15]Some have in fact already turned away to follow Satan.

[16]If any woman who is a believer has widows in her family, she should help them and not let the church be burdened with them, so that the church can help those widows who are really in need.

1) *What kind of good things do faithful widows do? Do we praise widows (and others) enough for the good they do?*

2) *Are the physical desires of young widows evil? If not, how are those desires to be expressed?*

3) *Do churches today intentionally care for widows, or do we leave that to the government? What things can the church do to care for older members?*

Day Three Reading and Questions:

[17]The elders who direct the affairs of the church well are worthy of double honor, especially those whose work is preaching and teaching. [18]For the Scripture says, "Do not muzzle the ox while it is treading out the grain," and "The worker deserves his wages." [19]Do not entertain an accusation against an elder unless it is brought by two or three witnesses. [20]Those who sin are to be rebuked publicly, so that the others may take warning.

[21]I charge you, in the sight of God and Christ Jesus and the elect angels, to keep these instructions without partiality, and to do nothing out of favoritism.

[22]Do not be hasty in the laying on of hands, and do not share in the sins of others. Keep yourself pure.

[23]Stop drinking only water, and use a little wine because of your stomach and your frequent illnesses.

> 1) *Should we pay ministers and other church workers? Does this make them employees of the church? Who do they really work for?*
>
> 2) *Why should there be two or three witnesses against an elder?*
>
> 3) *Paul tells Timothy to drink wine. Should we do so today? Why would Paul give such advice to Timothy?*

Day Four Reading and Questions:

[24]The sins of some men are obvious, reaching the place of judgment ahead of them; the sins of others trail behind them. [25]In the same way, good deeds are obvious, and even those that are not cannot be hidden.

[1]All who are under the yoke of slavery should consider their masters worthy of full respect, so that God's name and our teaching may not be slandered. [2]Those who have believing masters are not to show less respect for them because they are brothers. Instead, they are to serve them even better, because those who benefit from their service are believers, and dear to them. These are the things you are to teach and urge on them.

1) *Is it encouraging or frightening that our hidden sins and hidden good deeds will be brought to light?*

2) *When was the last time you did something good for someone and did not tell anyone? Is there greater virtue in these hidden good deeds?*

3) *Does the Bible approve of slavery? Why doesn't Paul condemn slavery? Shouldn't Christian slaves seek their freedom?*

DAY FIVE READING AND QUESTIONS:

Go back and read the entire passage.

1) *Should we treat everyone in church alike? If not, are we not playing favorites?*

2) *What is our responsibility to our families? To our church families?*

3) *Do ministers often show favoritism? If so, to what groups?*

MEDITATION ON 1 TIMOTHY 5:1-6:2

We live in an age where youth is prized. Both men and women spend billions of dollars each year on cosmetics, hair color, and plastic surgery in order to look younger. We exercise not primarily for health (although that's what we tell ourselves) but to maintain a youthful appearance. On television and in magazines, we see nothing but fresh faces—even the old actors look young!

We live in an age where being old means having less value. Old people drive slow, move slow, think slow. They should just retire and get out of the way. Having them around reminds us that we too might get old someday. We don't want to admit that.

We live in the age of individual rights. What is important is my own self-fulfillment and the happiness of my family. Family meaning mom, dad, and the kids. Taking care of grandma or grandpa would seriously cramp our lifestyle.

As Christians, we are called to stand against the powers of our age. While others ignore or dismiss older people, we lovingly care for them. We treat older men as fathers and older women as mothers. We care for our own aged mothers and fathers, even if it costs us. Even if it inconveniences us. Even if it cuts into our lifestyle.

Older people are a treasure for the church, a treasure we neglect to our own harm. Older men and women have a wealth of experience, a surplus of time, and a heart for service that the church desperately needs. We dare not marginalize those whom our world devalues— older people, women, and the poor—for to such belong the kingdom of God.

"Father, give us love and appreciation for those our age does not appreciate. May we care for those in need even if it costs us. Remind us how much it cost you to love us."

THE TROUBLE WITH MONEY

(1 TIMOTHY 6:3-21)

DAY ONE READING AND QUESTIONS:

³If anyone teaches false doctrines and does not agree to the sound instruction of our Lord Jesus Christ and to godly teaching, ⁴he is conceited and understands nothing. He has an unhealthy interest in controversies and quarrels about words that result in envy, strife, malicious talk, evil suspicions ⁵and constant friction between men of corrupt mind, who have been robbed of the truth and who think that godliness is a means to financial gain.

⁶But godliness with contentment is great gain. ⁷For we brought nothing into the world, and we can take nothing out of it. ⁸But if we have food and clothing, we will be content with that. ⁹People who want to get rich fall into temptation and a trap and into many foolish and harmful desires that plunge men into ruin and destruction. ¹⁰For the love of money is a root of all kinds of evil. Some people, eager for money, have wandered from the faith and pierced themselves with many griefs.

1) *Where do quarrels about words lead? Have you seen such arguments in church? What can we do to prevent them?*

2) *Why is it so hard to be content with what we have? Shouldn't we want to have a little more money?*

3) *Do you want to be rich? Is this the same as the love of money?*

Day Two Reading and Questions:

[11]But you, man of God, flee from all this, and pursue righteousness, godliness, faith, love, endurance and gentleness. [12]Fight the good fight of the faith. Take hold of the eternal life to which you were called when you made your good confession in the presence of many witnesses. [13]In the sight of God, who gives life to everything, and of Christ Jesus, who while testifying before Pontius Pilate made the good confession, I charge you [14]to keep this command without spot or blame until the appearing of our Lord Jesus Christ, [15]which God will bring about in his own time—God, the blessed and only Ruler, the King of kings and Lord of lords, [16]who alone is immortal and who lives in unapproachable light, whom no one has seen or can see. To him be honor and might forever. Amen.

1) What should Timothy (and we) flee from? What should he (and we) pursue?

2) What is the importance of confessing before witnesses?

3) Why does Paul mention the Second Coming here?

Day Three Reading and Questions:

[17]Command those who are rich in this present world not to be arrogant nor to put their hope in wealth, which is so uncertain, but to put their hope in God, who richly provides us with everything for our enjoyment. [18]Command them to do good, to be rich in good deeds, and to be generous and willing to share. [19]In this way they will lay up treasure for themselves as a firm foundation for the coming age, so that they may take hold of the life that is truly life.

1) *Why is it so easy to trust in riches? Do we trust in insurance, retirement accounts, and our bank balance? Or is our trust in God?*

2) *What are the rich to do with their money? Are we rich? What should we do with our money?*

3) *Does "lay up treasure" remind you of something Jesus said? Did Paul know the teaching of Jesus?*

Day Four Reading and Questions:

[20]Timothy, guard what has been entrusted to your care. Turn away from godless chatter and the opposing ideas of what is falsely called knowledge, [21]which some have professed and in so doing have wandered from the faith.

Grace be with you.

1) *What had been entrusted to Timothy? How should he guard it?*

2) *What is godless chatter? Give examples.*

3) *What does it mean to wander from the faith? Is this wandering intentional? How can it be prevented?*

Day Five Reading and Questions:

Go back and read the entire passage.

1) *Why does Paul talk so much about riches in this section? Is the Bible prejudiced against rich people? Shouldn't we want to be rich so we can help others?*

2) Are most church controversies really over "issues" or are they quarrels over power? Who should have power in the church?

3) Should godliness lead to financial gain? Can preachers make too much money? Should being a Christian help you be successful in your job or business?

MEDITATION ON 1 TIMOTHY 6:3-21

We can all look down on the rich. They ride in limousines, sail their yachts, and live in multi-million dollar mansions while ignoring the poor and oppressed.

We're glad we are not rich.

Or are we? Don't we want to be rich? Would we turn down the ten million dollar sweepstakes prize? Think of the good things we could do with that money! Feed the poor, house the homeless, support education. Oh yes, we could also pay off our debts and buy a new car and house for our family. We would be smart about it, putting enough in savings to care for us in retirement. We might even quit our jobs. We'd have it made.

Isn't that the American dream? Are we not bombarded each day with advertisements that promise youth, pleasure, happiness, and security for just a few dollars more? Isn't it foolish to be content with what you have when you could have more? But "wanting more" is just another word for greed.

And that's the frightening warning in this passage. It is not only for the rich, but for all who want to be rich. Not just the rich live in spiritual danger, those who want to be rich fall into many harmful desires. It is those eager for money who wander from the faith.

That eagerness for wealth can take over our imaginations, warp our hearts, and corrupt our minds. We can deceive ourselves into thinking others are rich, not us. As a student of mine once said (in all seriousness), "Rich people live in three-story houses. I live in a two-story house, so I'm not rich." Precisely. We define rich as those who have one more than we do. Thus, we never see ourselves as we are. We are the rich.

It is difficult for the average American to realize that compared to most of the world we are rich, and so the words to the rich are also for us. We will be exalted if we are rich, but only if we understand the low value of our wealth and the true value of faith. Only by humbly reception of the gift of God can the impossible happen; even the rich can be saved (Mark 10:27). Only by God's grace can we be truly rich, rich in good deeds and generosity.

"Lord, may we accept your demanding love and give up all to follow you, knowing that you alone are our treasure."

2 TIMOTHY: FOLLOWING JESUS IN THE LAST DAYS

THE SPIRITUALITY OF 2 TIMOTHY

This is a moving letter from Paul to his beloved Timothy, moving because Paul is about to be offered as a sacrifice to God (2 Timothy 4:6). By overhearing Paul's farewell address to his dear son in the faith, the Spirit moves us to be faithful to Jesus at all cost.

THE GOOD DEPOSIT

Paul urges Timothy to guard his faith like a treasure entrusted to him (2 Timothy1:14). A godly mother and grandmother (2 Timothy 1:5) passed down this faith to Timothy. Thus from his infancy he has known the God-breathed Scriptures that bring wisdom and profit (2 Timothy 3:14-16).

We too have received the marvelous gift of faith from those who love us—parents, brothers, sisters, and friends. Someone cared enough to teach us the marvelous story of Jesus, that trustworthy saying of a faithful Lord. We must hold fast to that faith, guarding it from all danger and opposition.

FAITHFULNESS IN TERRIBLE TIMES

That faith is especially precious and vulnerable in the terrible times of the last days. Selfishness, violence, and deceit surround us (2

Timothy 3:1-9). False teachers destroy the faith of some (2 Timothy 2:16-19). God's leaders are in chains. In such times, we are tempted to be ashamed of the Lord. Instead, Jesus calls us to live as soldiers, athletes, and farmers for the sake of Christ, knowing that our faithful service will someday be rewarded (2 Timothy 2:1-6).

The Help of the Spirit

But who has the strength to be faithful in such unseasonable times? We are likely to be timid and afraid on our own. But we are not alone. God gives us his Spirit to help us guard the good deposit of faith (2 Timothy 1:14). That Spirit is not one of timidity but one of power, love, and self-control (2 Timothy 1:7). Like Timothy, we must fan into flame the gift of God, proclaiming the great message of Jesus in season and out.

MEDITATIONS ON 2 TIMOTHY:

SPIRIT OF POWER

(2 TIMOTHY 1:1-2:7)

DAY ONE READING AND QUESTIONS:

¹Paul, an apostle of Christ Jesus by the will of God, according to the promise of life that is in Christ Jesus,

²To Timothy, my dear son: Grace, mercy and peace from God the Father and Christ Jesus our Lord.

³I thank God, whom I serve, as my forefathers did, with a clear conscience, as night and day I constantly remember you in my prayers. ⁴Recalling your tears, I long to see you, so that I may be filled with joy. ⁵I have been reminded of your sincere faith, which first lived in your grandmother Lois and in your mother Eunice and, I am persuaded, now lives in you also. ⁶For this reason I remind you to fan into flame the gift of God, which is in you through the laying on of my hands. ⁷For God did not give us a spirit of timidity, but a spirit of power, of love and of self-discipline.

1) Paul serves God as his forefathers did. Were not his forefathers Jews? Is Paul still a Jew or a Christian?

2) Who passed the faith on to you as Lois and Eunice did to Timothy? Are you thankful for that gift?

*3) Are we timid about the gift God has given us? Are we and our
churches ruled by fear or by a Spirit of power?*

DAY TWO READING AND QUESTIONS:

[8]So do not be ashamed to testify about our Lord, or ashamed of
me his prisoner. But join with me in suffering for the gospel, by the
power of God, [9]who has saved us and called us to a holy life—not
because of anything we have done but because of his own purpose
and grace. This grace was given us in Christ Jesus before the beginning
of time, [10]but it has now been revealed through the appearing of our
Savior, Christ Jesus, who has destroyed death and has brought life and
immortality to light through the gospel. [11]And of this gospel I was
appointed a herald and an apostle and a teacher. [12]That is why I am
suffering as I am. Yet I am not ashamed, because I know whom I have
believed, and am convinced that he is able to guard what I have
entrusted to him for that day.

*1) Why would Timothy be tempted to be ashamed of the Lord or of
Paul? Are we ever ashamed to be Christians? Why?*

2) Do we suffer for the gospel today? Should we? How?

*3) How does Paul know whom he has believed? What does he know
about him?*

DAY THREE READING AND QUESTIONS:

[13]What you heard from me, keep as the pattern of sound teaching,
with faith and love in Christ Jesus. [14]Guard the good deposit that was
entrusted to you—guard it with the help of the Holy Spirit who lives in us.
[15]You know that everyone in the province of Asia has deserted me,

including Phygelus and Hermogenes.

[16]May the Lord show mercy to the household of Onesiphorus, because he often refreshed me and was not ashamed of my chains. [17]On the contrary, when he was in Rome, he searched hard for me until he found me. [18]May the Lord grant that he will find mercy from the Lord on that day! You know very well in how many ways he helped me in Ephesus.

1) What is sound teaching? How do we recognize it?

2) What is the good deposit Timothy had received?

3) Who has refreshed you like Onesiphorus did Paul? Whom have you refreshed?

DAY FOUR READING AND QUESTIONS:

[1]You then, my son, be strong in the grace that is in Christ Jesus. [2]And the things you have heard me say in the presence of many witnesses entrust to reliable men who will also be qualified to teach others. [3]Endure hardship with us like a good soldier of Christ Jesus. [4]No one serving as a soldier gets involved in civilian affairs—he wants to please his commanding officer. [5]Similarly, if anyone competes as an athlete, he does not receive the victor's crown unless he competes according to the rules. [6]The hardworking farmer should be the first to receive a share of the crops. [7]Reflect on what I am saying, for the Lord will give you insight into all this.

1) How is a Christian like a soldier?

2) How is a Christian like an athlete?

3) How is a Christian like a farmer?

DAY FIVE READING AND QUESTIONS:

Go back and read the entire passage.

1) What makes our faith sincere? How do we show that sincerity?

2) How is the Holy Spirit a spirit of power? Give biblical examples.

*3) Besides a soldier, an athlete, and a farmer, what other occupations
can be compared to being a Christian?*

MEDITATION ON 2 TIMOTHY 1:1-2:7

Have we ever been embarrassed to be Christians? Embarrassed
because of what other Christians do? To many, "Christian" implies
narrow-minded, judgmental, and hypocritical. Embarrassed because
to admit you are a Christian may cost you approval and friendship?
Because it marks you as strange and different?

Timothy could have been embarrassed. After all, his friend Paul
was in jail for being a Christian. We generally are not proud of our
friends in jail! To associate too closely with Paul might mean jail time
for Timothy too.

What would we do in Timothy's shoes? What do we do when we
are embarrassed to be Christians? We might be tempted to downplay
our faith, to be quiet, timid Christians.

Instead, Paul reminds us of the Spirit we have received. God's
Spirit does not make us fearful or timid. Instead, he gives us power,
love, and self-discipline. Power to be bold in our Christianity in spite
of opposition. Power to guard the wonderful message we have
received. Love for those who oppose us, even those who desert us.

Self-control that enables us to be faithful soldiers, trained athletes, and hardworking farmers for the sake of Christ.

By the power of the Spirit we go from shame to boldness, knowing that our victory, our crown, and our harvest await us. In our time, as well as in Timothy's, what the world is waiting for is for Christians to shake off their timid fears and boldly live in the power of the Spirit.

"Father, give us your Spirit so we may be bold as Christians in our world."

REMEMBER JESUS CHRIST
(2 TIMOTHY 2:8-16)

Day One Reading and Questions:

⁸Remember Jesus Christ, raised from the dead, descended from David. This is my gospel, ⁹for which I am suffering even to the point of being chained like a criminal. But God's word is not chained. ¹⁰Therefore I endure everything for the sake of the elect, that they too may obtain the salvation that is in Christ Jesus, with eternal glory.

1) *Is Timothy apt to forget Jesus? Are we? Why do we need reminders of Jesus Christ?*

2) *Why is it significant that Jesus is descended from David? Why are the Old Testament stories important to Christians?*

3) *What does, "God's word is not chained" mean? How is that encouraging to us today? Is the power in the gospel or in who proclaims it?*

Day Two Reading and Questions:

¹¹Here is a trustworthy saying:
    If we died with him,
        we will also live with him;

[12]if we endure,

> we will also reign with him.
> If we disown him,
> he will also disown us;

[13]if we are faithless,

> he will remain faithful,
> for he cannot disown himself.

1) Aren't all biblical sayings trustworthy? Why does Paul introduce this poem or hymn by saying it is trustworthy?

2) How have we died with Christ? What keeps us from enduring in our faith? Why would we disown Jesus? Why would he disown us?

3) Why is God faithful when we are faithless? Is this an encouraging word to us?

DAY THREE READING AND QUESTIONS:

[14]Keep reminding them of these things. Warn them before God against quarreling about words; it is of no value, and only ruins those who listen. [15]Do your best to present yourself to God as one approved, a workman who does not need to be ashamed and who correctly handles the word of truth. [16]Avoid godless chatter, because those who indulge in it will become more and more ungodly. [17]Their teaching will spread like gangrene. Among them are Hymenaeus and Philetus, [18]who have wandered away from the truth. They say that the resurrection has already taken place, and they destroy the faith of some. [19]Nevertheless, God's solid foundation stands firm, sealed with this inscription: "The Lord knows those who are his," and, "Everyone who confesses the name of the Lord must turn away from wickedness."

1) How is Timothy like a workman? What does he work with? How does he handle it? How are we all like workers for God?

2) Why would anyone believe the resurrection had already taken place? Why is this a teaching destructive to faith?

3) "The Lord knows those who are his." Is this an encouraging word? A warning?

DAY FOUR READING AND QUESTIONS:

[20]In a large house there are articles not only of gold and silver, but also of wood and clay; some are for noble purposes and some for ignoble. [21]If a man cleanses himself from the latter, he will be an instrument for noble purposes, made holy, useful to the Master and prepared to do any good work.

[22]Flee the evil desires of youth, and pursue righteousness, faith, love and peace, along with those who call on the Lord out of a pure heart. [23]Don't have anything to do with foolish and stupid arguments, because you know they produce quarrels. [24]And the Lord's servant must not quarrel; instead, he must be kind to everyone, able to teach, not resentful. [25]Those who oppose him he must gently instruct, in the hope that God will grant them repentance leading them to a knowledge of the truth, [26]and that they will come to their senses and escape from the trap of the devil, who has taken them captive to do his will.

1) What is the point of the illustration about gold, silver, wood, and clay articles? Which does Paul want Timothy (and us) to be? How do we become that?

2) What is the difference between quarrelling and gently instructing those who oppose you?

3) *Earlier Paul called Hymenaeus and Philetus false teachers. Does Paul think even they might come to repentance or are they too far gone? Should we ever give up on false teachers?*

DAY FIVE READING AND QUESTIONS:

Go back and read the entire passage.

1) *Give examples of those who quarreled against other Christians, calling everyone who disagreed with them, "false teachers." Was this quarreling good for the church?*

2) *Should we be at all concerned about false teachers in the church? Can a church be too tolerant in their teaching?*

3) *We are all wrong about something. What is the difference between being wrong and being a false teacher?*

MEDITATION ON 2 TIMOTHY 2:8-26

Remember Jesus Christ.

Are we likely to forget him? Don't we know the old, old story of Jesus and his love? Of course we do! Many of us have known it all our lives. It's one of the first stories we heard. We hear the story at home and at church. We sing the story. We hear it preached and taught. We assume everyone knows it, so we don't tell it as we should. We may even grow tired of hearing the story. It does seem awfully old, at times.

Still, we need reminding. It's not that we will forget the story of Jesus or the gospel stories about him. The danger is that we will forget the impact of those stories. We will forget Jesus in temptation. We will forget him when we face the homeless by the side of the road. We will forget him at work, thinking he has no place there. We will forget him when others come along and tell what they think is a better story. We will live our lives by other stories—success stories, the American story, our personal stories.

We need to be reminded of Jesus.

Why do we need a reminder?

Because there are those who would twist and pervert the story of Jesus. They wander away from the truth and destroy the faith of others. They are not merely mistaken in doctrine, but in the way they live.

Warnings against false teaching may be wasted on many of us. We have heard so many Christians falsely accused of heresy that we have come to doubt there can be real false teaching. But false teachers abound in our day as well as in Timothy's. Many today would lead us away from our story.

What do we do about them? We do not ignore them, we confront them. But we do so with gentle firmness, in hope they will come back to God. After all, that is our story, the story of a God who wants all to come to him.

"God of love, remind us constantly of the great story of Jesus and his love. May we gently oppose those who lead others away from that story."

GOD-BREATHED SCRIPTURE
(2 TIMOTHY 3:1-17)

Day One Reading and Questions:

[1]But mark this: There will be terrible times in the last days.
[2]People will be lovers of themselves, lovers of money, boastful, proud, abusive, disobedient to their parents, ungrateful, unholy, [3]without love, unforgiving, slanderous, without self-control, brutal, not lovers of the good, [4]treacherous, rash, conceited, lovers of pleasure rather than lovers of God— [5]having a form of godliness but denying its power. Have nothing to do with them.

1) *Are we living in the last days? Does this description sound like our times?*

2) *What or who are the things people love in this description? What or who do they not love?*

3) *What does it mean to have a form of godliness? How can people appear godly who are described this way?*

Day Two Reading and Questions:

[6]They are the kind who worm their way into homes and gain control over weak-willed women, who are loaded down with sins and

are swayed by all kinds of evil desires, [7]always learning but never able to acknowledge the truth. [8]Just as Jannes and Jambres opposed Moses, so also these men oppose the truth—men of depraved minds, who, as far as the faith is concerned, are rejected. [9]But they will not get very far because, as in the case of those men, their folly will be clear to everyone.

1) *Are women more weak-willed than men? What does Paul mean here?*

2) *Is Paul opposed to education and learning? Does learning and education always lead to the truth?*

3) *Why will false teachers not get very far? If they won't get far, why does Paul warn so strongly against them?*

Day Three Reading and Questions:

[10]You, however, know all about my teaching, my way of life, my purpose, faith, patience, love, endurance, [11]persecutions, sufferings— what kinds of things happened to me in Antioch, Iconium and Lystra, the persecutions I endured. Yet the Lord rescued me from all of them. [12]In fact, everyone who wants to live a godly life in Christ Jesus will be persecuted, [13]while evil men and impostors will go from bad to worse, deceiving and being deceived.

1) *Why does Paul use himself as an example here? Is he bragging?*

2) *Are Christians persecuted today? Are all Christians persecuted? How?*

3) *How are evil men and imposters being deceived? What is so frightening about self-deception?*

Day Four Reading and Questions:

[14]But as for you, continue in what you have learned and have become convinced of, because you know those from whom you learned it, [15]and how from infancy you have known the holy Scriptures, which are able to make you wise for salvation through faith in Christ Jesus. [16]All Scripture is God-breathed and is useful for teaching, rebuking, correcting and training in righteousness, [17]so that the man of God may be thoroughly equipped for every good work.

1) *From whom had Timothy learned the Scriptures (see 2 Timothy 1:5)? How did that convince him of the truth of the Scriptures? Does it matter who teaches us the Bible?*

2) *What does it mean that the Scriptures are God-breathed or inspired?*

3) *What is Scripture useful for?*

Day Five Reading and Questions

Go back and read the entire passage.

1) *How do the Scriptures guard us from false teachers?*

2) *Are we told here exactly how the Bible is inspired? Should we argue over how they are inspired?*

3) *Why is knowing and practicing the Scriptures of particular importance in the last days?*

MEDITATION ON 2 TIMOTHY 3:1-17

All Christians respect the Bible. All believe it to be from God. All think Bible study is necessary for Christian growth.

Yet most of us neglect regular Bible study. Why? Because doing anything regularly is hard. Because we don't know how to study the Bible. Because we'd rather argue over how the Bible is inspired rather than profit from personal Bible study.

We rightly study the Bible for information. We ask, "Who wrote this?" "When was it written?" "Who were the original readers?" "How do these words apply to me?" More importantly, we want information about God. Who is he? What does he think of me? What does he want from me?

There is no substitute for this kind of close, dedicated Bible study. We must know what the Bible says to know our standing with God. We therefore read the Bible to discover true doctrine or teaching. But some, in their emphasis on the authority and inspiration of the Bible, have forgotten that Bible study is not an end in itself. We want to know God through Scripture. We want to have a relationship with the Teacher, not just the teachings.

Jesus tells some of God's people in his day, "You diligently study the Scriptures because you think that by them you possess eternal life. These are the Scriptures that testify about me, yet you refuse to come to me to have life" (John 5:39-40). He's not telling them to study their Bibles less, but he is reminding them of the deeper purpose of Bible study—to draw us to God through Jesus. Bible study is a means, not an end.

Reading the Bible is not like reading other books. We are not simply trying to learn information or master material. Instead, we want to stand under the authority of Scripture and let God master us. While we read the Bible, it reads us, opening the depths of our being to the overpowering love of God.

We particularly need that power in the terrible times of the last days. When deceivers are abroad, sticking closely to God's word gives us the courage to oppose them. It allows us to rebuke and correct. More importantly, Scripture trains us in righteousness, giving us both sound teaching and healthy living.

"Father, thank you for giving us the Scriptures. Thank you for those who taught us. May we live in the Scriptures and may they live in us."

IN SEASON AND OUT

(2 TIMOTHY 4:1-22)

Day One Reading and Questions:

¹In the presence of God and of Christ Jesus, who will judge the living and the dead, and in view of his appearing and his kingdom, I give you this charge: ²Preach the Word; be prepared in season and out of season; correct, rebuke and encourage—with great patience and careful instruction. ³For the time will come when men will not put up with sound doctrine. Instead, to suit their own desires, they will gather around them a great number of teachers to say what their itching ears want to hear. ⁴They will turn their ears away from the truth and turn aside to myths. ⁵But you, keep your head in all situations, endure hardship, do the work of an evangelist, discharge all the duties of your ministry.

1) *What does "out of season" mean? How do preachers preach out of season?*

2) *Give examples of how many today have itching ears and gather teachers who tell them what they want to hear. Would your church have a preacher who did not tell them what they wanted to hear?*

3) *What hardships must ministers endure? How can they keep their heads in those situations?*

DAY TWO READING AND QUESTIONS:

[6]For I am already being poured out like a drink offering, and the time has come for my departure. [7]I have fought the good fight, I have finished the race, I have kept the faith. [8]Now there is in store for me the crown of righteousness, which the Lord, the righteous Judge, will award to me on that day—and not only to me, but also to all who have longed for his appearing.

> *1) How is the Christian life like a fight or a race? Must we win the fight or race?*

> *2) Is it right to desire a crown from God? Should we serve God to get a reward? What is our reward for serving him?*

> *3) Do we long for the appearing of Jesus? What might make us long more for the Second Coming?*

DAY THREE READING AND QUESTIONS:

[9]Do your best to come to me quickly, [10]for Demas, because he loved this world, has deserted me and has gone to Thessalonica. Crescens has gone to Galatia, and Titus to Dalmatia. [11]Only Luke is with me. Get Mark and bring him with you, because he is helpful to me in my ministry. [12]I sent Tychicus to Ephesus. [13]When you come, bring the cloak that I left with Carpus at Troas, and my scrolls, especially the parchments.

[14]Alexander the metalworker did me a great deal of harm. The Lord will repay him for what he has done. [15]You too should be on your guard against him, because he strongly opposed our message.

1) *What does it mean that Demas loved this world? W can we keep ourselves from loving the world?*

2) *Why does Paul want scrolls and parchments? What does this tell you about him?*

3) *Should we want God to repay those who did us harm? Should we take vengeance against others?*

Day Four Reading and Questions:

[16]At my first defense, no one came to my support, but everyone deserted me. May it not be held against them. [17]But the Lord stood at my side and gave me strength, so that through me the message might be fully proclaimed and all the Gentiles might hear it. And I was delivered from the lion's mouth. [18]The Lord will rescue me from every evil attack and will bring me safely to his heavenly kingdom. To him be glory for ever and ever. Amen.

[19]Greet Priscilla and Aquila and the household of Onesiphorus. [20]Erastus stayed in Corinth, and I left Trophimus sick in Miletus. [21]Do your best to get here before winter. Eubulus greets you, and so do Pudens, Linus, Claudia and all the brothers.

[22]The Lord be with your spirit. Grace be with you.

1) *Have you ever been deserted by those who claimed to be your friends? Who is the friend Paul relied on?*

2) *What dangers face us as Christians? Are they as great as those Paul faced? Who will bring us safely through them?*

3) *Why does Paul want Timothy there before winter?*

DAY FIVE READING AND QUESTIONS:

Go back and read the entire passage.

1) What did it cost Paul to preach the gospel? What did it cost Timothy? What will it cost us?

2) Do we ever confront and rebuke others? Why do we find this so difficult? How can we be firm yet gentle with other Christians?

3) Should our emphasis as Christians be on winning at life or on being faithful?

MEDITATION ON 2 TIMOTHY 4:1-22

In season and out of season. There are definitely times when being a Christian is out of season.

It was that way for Paul. Being God's apostle did not mean fame and fortune for him. It meant persecution. It meant being poured out like a sacrifice. It even meant being deserted by those who claimed to be his brothers and sisters. "Everyone deserted me," he says. What sad words for one who was a faithful fighter.

Timothy would also experience days "out of season." All ministers do. Those who scratch the itching ears around them get much more of a hearing. They become the popular preachers with large congregations, big budgets, and visible success. Timothy and ministers like him are ignored. No matter. The call is to be faithful, to endure hardship, to not give up the fight especially when it looks as though you are losing.

All Christians experience "out of season" times. All who want to live godly will face persecution. Harsh words. Misunderstanding.

Blame. Some will even hate us because we show tough love to them. No matter. Be faithful anyway.

Is this a depressing message? No! Not at all. For no matter what others do or say, no matter how unpopular true Christianity is, the Lord will rescue us from every evil and bring us safely to him. The fight is hard. The race is long. But the crown awaits. Don't give up, even when it is out of season.

"Lord Jesus, you were faithful when all, even those dearest to you, abandoned you. Give us the trust and courage to be faithful out of season."

TITUS: JESUS RENEWS HIS CHURCH

THE SPIRITUALITY OF TITUS

At first glance, the Book of Titus seems to have little regarding spirituality. The Holy Spirit is mentioned only once in the letter. However, in its advice on how a church should grow deeper as well as in size, the letter constantly relies on God's grace as embodied in Jesus and experienced through the Holy Spirit. The spirituality of Titus is a muscular one. The emphasis is on doing good to others since God has shown goodness to us.

TAUGHT SPIRITUALITY

The old adage is that Christianity must be caught, not taught. In many ways, Titus agrees with that, since the teaching here is not simply passing on information but is embodied, lived-out teaching. Healthy teaching (or sound doctrine) produces a healthy church. Leaders, ministers, older men and women, and even the young teach one another how to live in Christ. Ultimately, the grace of God himself is our teacher.

WORKING SPIRITUALITY

Titus is full of instruction on how to live as Christians, doing good to all around.

Doing good in this context is very different from "do-gooders" who meddle in the affairs of others. A healthy church knows when and how to rebuke those who need correction (Titus 1:13), but also slanders no one, is peaceable, and lives humbly in light of the kindness and love of God (Titus 3:1-5). Doing good means providing for oneself and family, but also for the needs of others (Titus 3:14).

RENEWAL SPIRITUALITY

Renewal is what the church needs most in our time as well as in the time of Titus. Our baptisms were times of renewal and reception of the Holy Spirit of God. The Spirit has been poured out by Jesus to produce healthy, taught, and working churches that bring the healing of Jesus to societies as sick as ancient Crete or contemporary America. Spiritual renewal will begin in our churches and in our society through the work of godly leaders who by the Spirit lovingly pass on the faith through word and through deeds.

MEDITATIONS ON TITUS

GOOD LEADERS

(TITUS 1:1-16)

Day One Reading and Questions:

¹Paul, a servant of God and an apostle of Jesus Christ for the faith of God's elect and the knowledge of the truth that leads to godliness—²a faith and knowledge resting on the hope of eternal life, which God, who does not lie, promised before the beginning of time, 3and at his appointed season he brought his word to light through the preaching entrusted to me by the command of God our Savior,

⁴To Titus, my true son in our common faith: Grace and peace from God the Father and Christ Jesus our Savior.

1) How often do we describe ourselves as "elect"? What does it mean to be chosen by God? Do we usually emphasize his choice of us or our choice to follow him? What does that imply about our faith?

2) How do faith, knowledge, godliness, and hope relate? Do we sometimes separate these blessings from one another? What happens when we do?

3) Think of those who mentored you in the faith. Share one of those stories with others. Is there someone you are mentoring in faith? Is there someone you should influence?

DAY TWO READING AND QUESTIONS:

[5]The reason I left you in Crete was that you might straighten out what was left unfinished and appoint elders in every town, as I directed you. [6]An elder must be blameless, the husband of but one wife, a man whose children believe and are not open to the charge of being wild and disobedient. [7]Since an overseer is entrusted with God's work, he must be blameless—not overbearing, not quick-tempered, not given to drunkenness, not violent, not pursuing dishonest gain. [8]Rather he must be hospitable, one who loves what is good, who is self-controlled, upright, holy and disciplined. [9]He must hold firmly to the trustworthy message as it has been taught, so that he can encourage others by sound doctrine and refute those who oppose it.

1) *The leaders here are called "elders" and "overseers." What do these two terms mean? What do they imply about the character of these leaders?*

2) *Twice these leaders are described as "blameless." What does this mean? Does it mean no one can blame them for anything? Does it imply perfection?*

3) *What seems to be the primary role of these leaders? What is it they are supposed to do?*

DAY THREE READING AND QUESTIONS:

[10]For there are many rebellious people, mere talkers and deceivers, especially those of the circumcision group. [11]They must be silenced, because they are ruining whole households by teaching things they ought not to teach—and that for the sake of dishonest gain. [12]Even

one of their own prophets has said, "Cretans are always liars, evil brutes, lazy gluttons." [13]This testimony is true. Therefore, rebuke them sharply, so that they will be sound in the faith [14]and will pay no attention to Jewish myths or to the commands of those who reject the truth.

1) What exactly was the circumcision group? Are they around today? Are rebellious talkers and deceivers around today?

2) Why do these teachers teach what they do? Are there preachers and teachers today who teach for the same reason?

3) Is your church a difficult church? Is it as much a challenge as Crete? Should we stay in difficult churches or look for better ones? What would Titus do?

Day Four Reading and Questions:

[15]To the pure, all things are pure, but to those who are corrupted and do not believe, nothing is pure. In fact, both their minds and consciences are corrupted. [16]They claim to know God, but by their actions they deny him. They are detestable, disobedient and unfit for doing anything good.

1) What part do our minds and consciences play in our perception of the world?

2) Can the same thing be "pure" to one person and not pure to another? How? Aren't things right or wrong in themselves?

3) Give examples today of leaders, teachers, and preachers who claim to know God but deny him by their actions. What is the warning here for us?

DAY FIVE READING AND QUESTIONS:

Go back and read the entire passage

1) Titus is told to rebuke these false teachers sharply. Do we hear much rebuking in church today? Why or why not? What are good and bad ways to rebuke?

2) Describe some good church leaders you have known. Describe some who did harm by their leadership. What is the key difference between these two groups?

3) Is this description of church leaders a legalistic checklist? Is it a description of character? What should we look for in leaders? How should we choose them?

MEDITATION ON TITUS 1:1-16

Titus faced a lost society. Lost in every sense of the word. Without morals. Without direction. Without hope. The same kind of society we increasingly find ourselves in. We live in a culture that not only is lost, but at times seems proud of it. What complicates matters for Titus and for us, are those who claim to be Christians and speak for God but who intentionally lead others astray to line their own pockets.

At first, this description of the Cretan church may seem irrelevant to our situation. How many people do you know from "the circumcision group"? But even if we don't face the exact same teaching today, we do face religious teachers who ruin whole families for dishonest gain. How many poor families have sent their hard-earned money to preachers promising health and wealth? How many churches have been split by power plays from leaders who want control of the finances? Mere talkers who preach but do not practice are still with us.

What do we do about them? Titus is told to rebuke them sharply. "Rebuking" does not come naturally to most of us. Our society and our churches are live-and-let-live. It's bad manners to correct someone. But if that someone is destroying whole families, can we afford not to confront them. Perhaps some of us came from oppressive religious backgrounds where church members were publicly rebuked for every minor fault. That's not what this passage recommends. Those to be condemned here are not just mistaken; they are intentionally deceiving the gullible for money, all in the name of Christ! If they are not stopped, the whole church suffers and outsiders bad-mouth the name of Christ.

How bad are these false Christians? Their description gets even uglier. "To the pure all things are pure, but to those who are corrupted and do not believe, nothing is pure. In fact, both their minds and consciences are corrupted. They claim to know God, but by their actions they deny him. They are detestable, disobedient and unfit for doing anything good" (Titus 1:15-16).

These are members of the Cretan church. Or at least they claim to be. What is God's plan for church growth? It doesn't depend on good material. One does not have to have a perfect church. The Cretan church had false teachers. Growth does not depend on a receptive society. Cretans were liars, evil beasts, lazy gluttons. No, true church growth depends on the power of God working through faithful leaders like Titus. Leaders who know when to encourage the fainthearted and when to rebuke the deceivers. Leaders who rely on the eternal purposes and promises of God. God's plan for church growth is for a church of ministers and missionaries who fight mere talkers by living the truth of Jesus.

Good leaders. That's the first step.

"God of wisdom, give us wise leaders who will encourage and rebuke in love. Help us to be those kind of leaders. May we lead by serving as Jesus himself did."

GOOD LEARNERS

(TITUS 2:1-15)

DAY ONE READING AND QUESTIONS:

¹You must teach what is in accord with sound doctrine. ²Teach the older men to be temperate, worthy of respect, self-controlled, and sound in faith, in love and in endurance.

³Likewise, teach the older women to be reverent in the way they live, not to be slanderers or addicted to much wine, but to teach what is good.

1) *What does sound doctrine mean? Why might the words "sound doctrine" leave a bad taste in our mouths? What is genuinely healthy teaching?*

2) *Why might it be difficult for Titus to teach older men? Is it easy to learn from those younger than we?*

3) *Think of some older women who shaped your faith. What debt do you owe them?*

DAY TWO READING AND QUESTIONS:

⁴Then they can train the younger women to love their husbands and children, ⁵to be self-controlled and pure, to be busy at home, to be

kind, and to be subject to their husbands, so that no one will malign the word of God.

⁶Similarly, encourage the young men to be self-controlled. ⁷In everything set them an example by doing what is good. In your teaching show integrity, seriousness ⁸and soundness of speech that cannot be condemned, so that those who oppose you may be ashamed because they have nothing bad to say about us.

1) *Why are older women to teach younger women? Was this only for the culture Titus knew or is it true today? What can women teach women that men cannot teach women?*

2) *The young women are to be trained to love their husbands and children. Can one be trained to love? How? What does this imply about the meaning of Christian love?*

3) *Why is self-control the only thing mentioned here that young men must be taught?*

DAY THREE READING AND QUESTIONS:

⁹Teach slaves to be subject to their masters in everything, to try to please them, not to talk back to them, ¹⁰and not to steal from them, but to show that they can be fully trusted, so that in every way they will make the teaching about God our Savior attractive.

1) *Does the Bible approve of slavery? Shouldn't Christian oppose slavery? Why does Paul not tell slaves to rebel and seek their rights and freedom?*

2) *Why should Christian slaves be hard working, trustworthy, and honest?*

3) Are their parallels to slavery in our current situation? What happens if we are stuck in a job where our boss is like a master and we feel like a slave? What should we do in that situation?

DAY FOUR READING AND QUESTIONS:

[11]For the grace of God that brings salvation has appeared to all men. [12]It teaches us to say "No" to ungodliness and worldly passions, and to live self-controlled, upright and godly lives in this present age, [13]while we wait for the blessed hope—the glorious appearing of our great God and Savior, Jesus Christ, [14]who gave himself for us to redeem us from all wickedness and to purify for himself a people that are his very own, eager to do what is good.

[15]These, then, are the things you should teach. Encourage and rebuke with all authority. Do not let anyone despise you.

1) What does it mean that grace has appeared to all people? Does this mean all will be saved?

2) We usually think of grace as forgiveness of sins. What does grace do here that goes beyond forgiveness?

3) What is hope? What is our hope?

DAY FIVE READING AND QUESTIONS:

Go back and read the entire passage.

1) Who is the teacher behind all the other teachers in this chapter?

2) Can Christianity be taught? Is this merely head knowledge or is another type of teaching and knowledge at work here?

3) Beyond using words, how else is Titus to teach in this chapter?

MEDITATION ON TITUS 2:1-15

"Sound doctrine" might leave a bad taste in our mouths. What some call "standing for sound doctrine" is just an excuse for controlling others who disagree with us. Such "sound doctrine" will be condemned later in Titus as foolish arguments.

But there is genuine sound doctrine, healthy teaching that is passed on not just by elders but by others. Older women pass them on to younger women. And not just to other women. Why do I believe in God? Many reasons, but it all boils down to this: my faith depends on the lives of godly women who passed the faith down to me. Not only older women but older men embodied the good news of Jesus for me. Bill Holloway (my dad), H.A. Fincher, Jr., Carl McKelvey, and others. Titus mentions younger men and women as learners, but they too can be teachers. At Lipscomb University, I have the best job in the world. They pay me to learn from my students! They teach me a depth of spiritual devotion that I did not have at their age.

What is God's plan for church growth? Healthy teaching. Teaching as Jesus taught, by making disciples. Healthy teaching is living by faith and calling others to join us on our faith journeys.

The ultimate teacher is God himself, a God of love who by his grace forgives our sins and reconciles us to him. But this is no cheap grace. It cost God his Son. It is a grace that demands we surrender all to God. It is a grace that accepts me "Just as I am", but will not leave me just as I am. This grace teaches us to wait. To wait hopefully, and patiently. To live self-controlled, upright, and godly lives. This is the healthy teaching God gives through elders, and through men and women who embody the grace of God.

"God of grace, teach us by your grace. Open our ears to hear your voice through godly men and women. Give us grace to teach others."

GOOD TEACHING
(TITUS 3:1-15)

DAY ONE READING AND QUESTIONS:

¹Remind the people to be subject to rulers and authorities, to be obedient, to be ready to do whatever is good, ²to slander no one, to be peaceable and considerate, and to show true humility toward all men.

³At one time we too were foolish, disobedient, deceived and enslaved by all kinds of passions and pleasures. We lived in malice and envy, being hated and hating one another.

1) Are most of the important teachings from God new to us? Why do we need to be reminded of what we already know?

2) What is humility? How is it different from low esteem?

3) Why does Paul remind us of how we used to be, before Jesus? How does this relate to humility? To being peaceable and considerate?

DAY TWO READING AND QUESTIONS:

⁴But when the kindness and love of God our Savior appeared, ⁵he saved us, not because of righteous things we had done, but because of his mercy. He saved us through the washing of rebirth and renewal by

the Holy Spirit, [6]whom he poured out on us generously through Jesus Christ our Savior, [7]so that, having been justified by his grace, we might become heirs having the hope of eternal life. [8]This is a trustworthy saying. And I want you to stress these things, so that those who have trusted in God may be careful to devote themselves to doing what is good. These things are excellent and profitable for everyone.

1) Why did God save us?

2) What is the washing of rebirth and renewal by the Holy Spirit? What other Bible verses connect washing and the Spirit?

3) What is the relationship between salvation and doing what is good? Do good works earn salvation? If not, why should we do them?

DAY THREE READING AND QUESTIONS:

[9]But avoid foolish controversies and genealogies and arguments and quarrels about the law, because these are unprofitable and useless. [10]Warn a divisive person once, and then warn him a second time. After that, have nothing to do with him. [11]You may be sure that such a man is warped and sinful; he is self-condemned.

1) What foolish controversies have divided the church in our day? How could those controversies have been avoided?

2) What should we do about someone in the church who likes to argue and threatens to divide the church? Have we let such people control the church? How can we stop that?

3) What does divisiveness say about a person's spiritual health?

Day Four Reading and Questions:

[12]As soon as I send Artemas or Tychicus to you, do your best to come to me at Nicopolis, because I have decided to winter there. [13]Do everything you can to help Zenas the lawyer and Apollos on their way and see that they have everything they need. [14]Our people must learn to devote themselves to doing what is good, in order that they may provide for daily necessities and not live unproductive lives.

[15]Everyone with me sends you greetings. Greet those who love us in the faith.

Grace be with you all.

1) How does your church supply the needs of traveling missionaries like Zenas and Apollos?

2) Why is there so much emphasis on doing what is good in this letter? Do we emphasize good works enough today?

3) What does a productive Christian life look like?

Day Five Reading and Questions:

Go back and read the entire passage.

1) The Holy Spirit is only mentioned once in Titus. What does the Spirit do for us according to this passage? Is the work of the Spirit implied elsewhere in Titus, although the word is not mentioned?

2) What is the relationship among the Spirit, healthy teaching, and doing good works?

3) How is Titus a model for growing healthy churches in a difficult environment? What can your church learn from this model?

MEDITATION ON TITUS 3:1-15

Most healthy teaching is not "brand new" but a reminder of what we already know. Here, Paul reminds us to treat outsiders (seekers) with consideration and humility. Such humility comes from remembering how far we have come by God's grace. We once were outsiders and were saved solely by the kindness, love and mercy of God. This keeps us from making evangelism into superiority and turning the good news of the gospel into the bad news of condemnation.

Also, sound doctrine (healthy teaching) is not arguing but avoiding foolish controversies. The most faithful teacher is not the one who judges other's motives and stirs up Christian against Christian. This is not healthy but destructive to the body of Christ.

But how can we build healthy churches out of "liars, evil beasts, and lazy gluttons?" How can a church grow when rebellious talkers and deceivers are in the church? How can we reach outsiders?

By remembering that a church rarely grows beyond the spiritual depth of its leaders. Our churches need to grow deeper. That only happens when leaders and members daily walk with God. It only happens when we daily walk with those who embody God. It only happens through the Spirit who continues to renew us through our baptisms.

This is God's plan for church growth. Good Ministers. Good Leaders. Good Followers. Who are taught by grace and who teach by grace.

"God our Savior, you saved us solely by your mercy and grace. Continue to renew us through your Spirit, removing any spirit of controversy. Remind us of your mercy, so we will humbly show mercy to others."

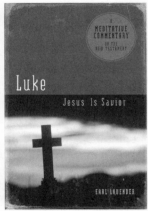
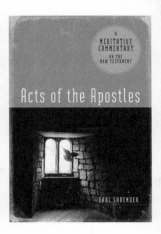
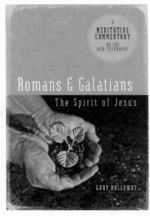